LEADERSHIP
From **Eden** to **Eternity**

LEADERSHIP
From Eden to Eternity

BISHOP PAUL MUTUA

Published by Sahel Publishing Association,
a subsidiary of Sahel Books Inc.
P.O. Box 21232 – 00505
Nairobi, Kenya
Tel: +011-254-715-596-106
For questions and orders log on to:
www.sahelpublishing.net

A Sahel Book
Nairobi. New Delhi. London. Charleston, Seattle
Editor: Sam Okello
Interior and cover designed by Hellen Wahonya Okello
Printed in India

To Pastors

Table of Contents

FOREWORD

It is with much pleasure I write this foreword to the book of one of the pioneers and pillars of the Pentecostal Movement in East Africa, Bishop Paul Mutua.

I believe I am the longest and closest living witness of his life as a convert, his baptism in the Holy Spirit, the Call, his ministry, his marriage and family.

We met in the city of Kampala over fifty years ago, as young entrepreneurs who loved the LORD. We then joined of the New Move of GOD, of HIS outpouring of HOLY SPIRIT, in Kampala, which had come through a Canadian Missionary. We were among the first converts and the first candidates baptized by immersion in the Kabaka's lake in Kampala.

Later we both abandoned our jobs and journeyed West to Fort Portal, in the Kingdom of Toro. Without knowing anyone, and with no financial support from the Elim Missionary Assemblies, we left for the place. We *pioneered* and built Pentecostal Churches in that region.

Bishop Mutua has proved to be a man of integrity, consumed with seeking the LORD in fasting and prayers, burdened by the lost souls, working tirelessly to preach, teach and make disciples for CHRIST his Master. Bishop Mutua – as I have known him over the years – is a man anointed of God, a man of deep faith with the great vision of building the Kingdom of God.

I am, therefore, not ashamed to highly recommend his book, which will challenge and inspire anyone reading it to walk in the Lord and the ministry for GOD.

To borrow the words of the Apostle Paul, I say *follow Bishop Mutua as he follows CHRIST.*

Bishop Dr. Charles Muyu
Gospel Tabernacle Churches of Kenya
Charles Muyu Ministries Inc. (USA)

PROLOGUE

On the day I looked at the railway line and asked where it ended, I had no idea it was a question inspired by God. I was tired and broken down and didn't know what else to do to turn my life around. Born into an Eastern Kenya home, where poverty and hopelessness and despair were the order of the day, I had endured my fair share of pain, felt the incredible power of *lack*. Forced to leave home or face starvation to death, I had finally gone to Kibwezi and was hired in the sprawling DWA sisal plantation. But my heart wasn't settled. I wanted to get as far away from poverty and my ruined home as possible. I wanted to leave the sorrows of my childhood behind, to say goodbye forever to the torment of going to bed in an empty stomach.

Like most people my age – and born into dire *circumstances* similar to mine – I don't know when I was born. Records in government books indicated 1942 as the date of my birth, but based on oral history of the time, and the state of my frailty today, I would say I arrived in this world in the late thirties. I'm told there was ululation and great jubilation when I was born because a son was born into the home of Mboko Kitonyi and his wife Wayua.

My dad and mom were poor in the extreme, but their state of lack did not stop them from celebrating my arrival. A son was a symbol of continuity in the African culture and thus I came with the guarantee that our family name would live on even after the death of my parents. Perhaps it was in realization of this that I was given the name *Ndisii* or District Commissioner – to signify the role my parents envisioned for me to play when I grew up.

Each time I think of that name today, I get amazed by the power of vision and hope. In spite of the grueling poverty in my home, my parents believed in the power of a better day, in the ability of their toddler to one day grow up and turn the fortunes of the home around. They were the two dreamers of the east, a husband and his wife who believed a better day was coming because a son was born.

As I grew up, though, I failed to share the optimism of my parents. I was young by the time my eyes opened to the horror of poverty around me, but they opened wide enough for me to sense the danger my family was in.

Food was in short supply, water was a scarce resource and milk was reserved for special occasions.

The clothes I wore were torn, dirty or too big for me. I wore them to the *ithembeo* or places of worship, where the community gathered to seek the urgent intervention of *Ngai Mwatuangi* or the god who split fingers, in times of great peril like prolonged droughts, epidemics and deaths of an inexplicable nature. Libations were poured and sacrifices made to appease the gods, who were feared to have occasioned the suffering of the people on account of something wrong the community had done.

In 1952, at the height of the clamor for independence, I got tired of the endless poverty at home and decided to go to school. The Colonial District Education Board, on the insistence of area Councilor Joel Kiteke Mbevete, started Matooni Primary School in my village. I went to school in a *shuka* even though the requirement was to wear a shirt and a pair of shorts. My father could not afford the shirt and he couldn't afford the pair of shorts either.

I stayed in school through the mercy of the teacher, Mr. Peter Mavui Sumbi. With time, though, he could no longer accept my situation and demanded that I either come to school in uniform or stop coming at all. Matters were not helped by the fact that Dad could not pay my fees either. When I got home one afternoon and told him I could no longer go to school in my *shuka*, he said, "The same *shuka* you wear is the one you sleep in!"

And indeed Dad led by example on this. He had one blanket that he wore during the day and slept in at night. He had nothing else to wear. His was a world where one woke up to seek the pleasure of illicit brew and spent the rest of the day in a state of daze. There was nothing he did of a profitable nature and nothing he did to change the state of his life. He was trapped in poverty forever!

But the worst was yet to come!

It came on the cold morning my mother died and I was left alone with my father. It went straight downhill from there. My life became a burden I was going to carry alone as Dad got lost in his drinking habit. As I look back today, I am stunned by the pattern that emerges when I weave the narrative of my life. The confounding tragedies and the uplifting moments fit together like a jigsaw puzzle and tell of the existence of the hand of God in my life since I was but a child in the dry bushes of a village deep in the tropical jungles of Africa.

the ultimate judgement on leadership will always be made far from the realms below – it will be made in heaven.

By the grace of God, I have set out to *decode* the encrypted codes of leadership – a matter that has eluded scholars, preachers and philosophers of all ages. In the spirit with which God has whispered these deep secrets to me, I bring them to you unadulterated.

May it be said of me one day, when I am dead and gone, that I lived my life in accordance with the revelation God entrusted me; and may I, like the Apostle Paul, one day say, "[7] I have fought a good fight, I have finished my course, I have kept the faith:[8] Henceforth there is laid up for me a crown of righteousness, which the Lord, the righteous judge, shall give me at that day: and not to me only, but unto all them also that love his appearing" (2 Timothy 4:7-8, KJV).

ONE

ANOINTMENT TO LEAD

I got into a train bound for Kampala, Uganda. Two years earlier, I had left Kibwezi and relocated to Kajiado, where the more promising job of a great quarry worker beckoned. I worked in Kajiado for a while and even contemplated going on to Nairobi, but from what I was told, Nairobi was too close to Matooni, where poverty had wrecked my life and my mom's grave slept silently as a testament to the helplessness of my wounded childhood. Rather than go to cold Nairobi to seek greener pastures, therefore, I stood by the winding iron line and asked a friend where the railway ended.

He said Kampala.

I didn't tell him why I asked, but I suspected he sensed my intention to leave Kajiado. For those who interacted with me at that time, my restlessness was always evident. I was a man running away from a past buried in poverty. I was a warrior who had decided to run away from hopelessness and make something of my life. I didn't know the God of the Salvation Army people who had pitched tent in Matooni village – and didn't recognize that still voice that had once whispered in my ear that *God does not sleep or slumber* – but I could tell that since I left my home, there was a force that had guided and protected and watched over me. That force had become my father and mother and would lead me away from perilous paths.

I can't say that on the day I pulled out my savings of two hundred shillings it was the friendly force that had asked me to get into a train and head to Kampala, but I know that once on that train, I became scared and wanted to feel closer to the force, to know what it was, to confide in it. The loneliness I experienced as I left Kajiado and headed to Kampala was so intense that for a while I wondered why I was doing something nobody else had ever done.

Was I normal?

The train made its way through the winding bushes and hills of Western Kenya, the plains of Uganda and finally reached Kampala. In that city, my first contact was a Luo man I bumped on in the hotel I had checked into the previous night. Without hesitation, I told him to ask the hotel owner if he knew of any Kambas in the city.

"There's one murram loader for a tractor company who passes by each evening from work," he said. "I'm sure he will today too."

With nothing else to do, I decided I would wait for that Kamba man who had become a carpenter in Kampala. He was going to become my host and guide on life in Uganda. In the evening, the man showed up for sure and he turned out to be a social drinker whose real name was John Mwaka, but went by the curious name Johnny Walker.

John took me in and we worked together for a while, but I eventually decided to move on to a better paying job in a construction site. One day, the supervisor found a friend and I sleeping on the roof of the building we were building and fired us on the spot. When I got home and told John about it, we agreed that it was time for us to start our own business. We thus got into a *charcoal* dealing business. In this business, the money was good and we managed to expand our reach into Eldoret, in Kenya, but there was an emptiness that gnawed at me.

It felt like a floating kite.

Controlled by remote.

Dry to the bone.

Dead!

Suddenly a powerful group associated with the Pentecostal Evangelistic Fellowship of Africa (PEFA) moved into the neighborhood, where our thriving charcoal business was located, and started preaching the word of God. There was a Rwandese evangelist in the group who made it a point to stop by our premises to invite us to the *evangelistic* meetings. He did so because I was tall and light-skinned, which made him think I was Rwandese too.

One day I woke up determined to go to the meetings and find out what the Canadian minister was preaching about. Was his message different from that of the Salvation Army team back in my village in Kenya? Was His white God more powerful than the gods of the *ithembeos* of Matooni? Could His God split fingers like Ngai *mwatuangi* could? If He could, I was willing to listen.

I went to the meeting that evening and the following Sunday went to church. It was while in that church that I prayed the sinner's prayer (Romans 10:8-9; 13 (KJV):

> [8] But what saith it? The word is nigh thee, even in thy mouth, and in thy heart: that is, the word of faith, which we preach; [9] That if thou shalt confess with thy

mouth the Lord Jesus, and shalt believe in thine heart that God hath raised him from the dead, thou shalt be saved. ...[13] For whosoever shall call upon the name of the Lord shall be saved.

That Sunday, I gave my life to the Lord and for the first time started to make the connection between the God the Canadian missionary was talking about and the powerful force that had kept me safe since I left home. That force, I now knew, was called God. God was the mighty force that had led me to Kibwezi, where I learnt to read and write, and He was the same force that had led me into a train that had brought me to Kampala. The question I now had to grapple with was – what was I going to do with this God who had now revealed Himself to me?

The Call

God didn't take long to answer that question. By this time I had dropped the charcoal business and owned a thriving hotel in Kampala. I experienced the favor of God as many of the city's elite gathered at my hotel to cut deals or socialize. I also noted that many ladies threw themselves at me, aware I was making good money, but the Lord kept me pure and guided me in the paths of righteousness. Then one night, as I slept, I felt wind on my mouth, like it was coming from the east. I woke up in shock and looked around, but there was nobody else with me – and the windows were firmly shut. Stunned by this encounter, I prayed and waited till morning. As soon as the sun lifted its head across the horizon, I went to Pastor Simon and asked what the wind from the east was about.

"Was it a dream?" he asked.

"I don't know, Pastor!"

"And you say it was at night?"

"Dead of the night, yes!"

Pastor Simon sensed at once what was going on. Like little Samuel of Shiloh, he realized that the Lord was calling me to carry the soothing message of salvation on my lips to a broken world. He, thus, told me to consider giving the Lord my full attention and letting Him lead in my life.

I accepted that wise counsel and presented myself to the Senior Pastor of Full Gospel Mission, Hugh Reg Layzell. The man of God prayed with me, then gave me the very first assignment I was to handle as one who had accepted the call of the Lord to service. He made me a storekeeper at the church. Since that humble beginning, I have walked with the Lord hand in hand, going to places and regions of the world I never would have imagined the son of a poor drunkard – an uneducated boy from a humble village of peasant farmers – going to sow the seed.

In the church – as in secular leadership today – I have been a witness to the tremendous struggles ministers of the gospel, officials in the government and those in the corporate world go through. I have seen great presidents in the United States face the torment of moral stain, celebrated leaders in the corporate world tumble and fall into ignominy, and *highly respected* church leaders collapse under the weight of the seductive influences of modern-day Delilahs. In my desire to understand the difference between those who remain faithful to the end and those who succumb to man's fallen nature, I have looked deeply into the matter of the call and the matter of anointing.

It is critical that we attune ourselves to the manner in which the Lord calls the servants He wants to lead His people whether as the president of a nation, as the chief of general staff of a great military, as a spiritual father or even as the head of a corporation whose essential products affect millions of lives around the world.

In the biblical book of Exodus, we come face to face with the deeper meaning of each call God places to man. The power of His voice, the urgency of His command and the clarity of the mission is unmistakable – because the stakes, when He calls, cannot be any higher. This call was to Moses, as is narrated in Exodus 3:1-15, (NIV):

> Now Moses was tending the flock of Jethro his father-in-law, the priest of Midian, and he led the flock to the far side of the wilderness and came to Horeb, the mountain of God. [2] There the LORD appeared to him in flames of fire from within a bush. Moses saw that though the bush was on fire it did not burn up. [3] So Moses thought, "I will go over and see this strange sight – why the bush does not burn up."
>
> [4] When the LORD saw that he had gone over to look, God called to him from within the bush, "Moses! Moses!"
>
> And Moses said, "Here I am."
>
> [5] "Do not come any closer," God said. "Take off your sandals, for the place where you are standing is holy ground." [6] Then he said, "I am the God of your father, the God of Abraham, the God of Isaac and the God of Jacob." At this, Moses hid his face, because he was afraid to look at God.
>
> [7] The LORD said, "I have indeed seen the misery of my people in Egypt. I have heard them crying out because

of their slave drivers, and I am concerned about their suffering. [8] So I have come down to rescue them from the hand of the Egyptians and to bring them up out of that land into a good and spacious land, a land flowing with milk and honey – the home of the Canaanites, Hittites, Amorites, Perizzites, Hivites and Jebusites.

[9] And now the cry of the Israelites has reached me, and I have seen the way the Egyptians are oppressing them. [10] So now, go. I am sending you to Pharaoh to bring my people the Israelites out of Egypt."

[11] But Moses said to God, "Who am I that I should go to Pharaoh and bring the Israelites out of Egypt?"

[12] And God said, "I will be with you. And this will be the sign to you that it is I who have sent you: When you have brought the people out of Egypt, you will worship God on this mountain."

[13] Moses said to God, "Suppose I go to the Israelites and say to them, 'The God of your fathers has sent me to you,' and they ask me, 'What is his name?' Then what shall I tell them?"

[14] God said to Moses, "I AM WHO I AM. This is what you are to say to the Israelites: 'I AM has sent me to you.'"

[15] God also said to Moses, "Say to the Israelites, 'The LORD, the God of your fathers – the God of

Abraham, the God of Isaac and the God of Jacob – has
sent me to you.'

"This is my name forever, the name you shall call
me from generation to generation."

Each call that comes to mortal man from the Creator of
the universe is a deeply powerful moment. There are core
pillars of God's encounter with man that must not escape
our attention. They are critical in our ability to separate
God's call from calls inspired by the demonic world and
made to masquerade as God's call.

a. **God calls by name.** When He appeared to Moses,
He was in the form of fire, but He called the old
shepherd by name. Later, He appeared to Samuel
and called the little boy, asleep in a Shiloh temple,
by name. There are those who will claim that God
spoke directly in the days of old, but does not do it
today. They say He would never call anybody by
name today and whoever claims to have heard His
voice is delusional, crazy or sick. In my walk with
God, I have come to realize that when the Lord
comes down to make His call, He will call His
servants by name. This is because:

- God's desire is to make each servant He
calls realize that He knows him or her by

name and has not made a mistake. This is because He is aware of the force of a call, the enormous *significance* of being enlisted in the mighty army that has pushed the agenda of salvation through the ages. This is the reason He calls by name – it is to say You poor boy from Matooni, You despised prostitute, You stammering old shepherd of the Midian desert … you are the one I'm calling to work with me!

- God wants His servants to realize that He knows each more intimately than we realize. When He meets us in the desert, like He met Moses, or in the temple like He met Samuel, or on the road like He later met the Apostle Paul, He is not at all meeting a stranger; He indeed is meeting a servant He knows by *name*, by *character* and by *creation*. He is inviting a person He has molded through the years to fulfill a specific role that buttresses the great plan of salvation.

- God's inspiring desire is to make His servants realize that He is opening a new chapter in their lives – one characterized by intimacy, honesty, and urgency. He is telling them, *by calling their name,* that from that moment on their name has been enshrined on the great stone of the ages, where the names of Abraham, David, Isaac and the Apostle Paul are enshrined. The intimacy that exists between Christ and the servant becomes one of a loyal shepherd and His anointed lamb.

b. **God identifies Himself.** In all His appearances, the Lord has been gracious enough to identify Himself to His servants. He does this to avoid any chance of mistaken identity – because He is aware there are demonic forces who impersonate Him, who are out to confuse the flock by pretending to be God. In His wisdom, when the Lord makes *an appearance,* He introduces Himself by deep names Satan and demons lack the creativity to unearth. Sample this:

- When He appeared to Moses, He said He was YHWH or Jehovah; the ancient God Moses had grown up being taught was the deliverer of Israel.
- When He appeared to the Apostle Paul, as the apostle was on his way to Damascus to

persecute Christians, God said, "Saul, Saul, why are you persecuting me?" He went on to introduce Himself to Saul and Saul's name changed to Paul. We know that after that encounter, Paul's life was transformed and he became one of the most forceful voices in speaking for God.

- When He appeared to John the Revelator, He introduced Himself as the Alpha and Omega, the Beginning and the End, the Lord who was, is and will always be. This is what theological scholars have described as being *omnipotent*, *omniscient* and *omnipresent*. He is the indescribable God because we cannot comprehend who He is!

c. **God's mission is defined.** He does not call without giving very specific instructions, without defining the nature and scope of the mission ahead. If it is light, He will say so; if it is a tough assignment, He will warn that it won't be easy. He is not in the habit of releasing His servants into shocking and discouraging situations without preparing them.

- He warned Abraham that "I will bless those who bless you, and *whoever* curses you I will curse (Genesis 12:3, NIV). In other words, there were going to be troubled times ahead, with some *blessing* and others *cursing* Abraham.

- He warned Moses that Pharaoh was going to be a difficult monarch; and that great occurrences would have to take place in Egypt before He let the *Israelites* go. It later took ten plagues, including the death of the heir apparent, for the stubborn Pharaoh to let God's people go. God had warned Moses.

d. God provides courage and grace. The Lord knows the nature of the adversary we are up against. He is aware that we are in a war fought in the spiritual realm, where the ferocious battles fought behind the scenes are *hidden* from us. For each assignment, therefore, He provides the courage and grace we need to overcome all manner of tribulations. He throws a protective ring around us as we march to war because His angels are assigned to become our bodyguards when the revolutionary message of the Cross is painted on our lips. Consider this:

- Samuel was just but a little boy when the Lord called and asked him to break the painful news of God's rejection of the House of Eli the priest. The great courage the little boy had, to undertake this mission, could have only come from God.
- David was a shepherd, out in the grazing fields, when the Lord plucked him out of obscurity and set his feet firmly in the heat of the battlefield. God provided the grace and courage the boy needed, which enabled him to use a sling and one smooth stone to bring down the Philistine giant.
- Jesus Christ, God's own son, cried in agony in the Garden of Gethsemane. The cross was before Him and the darkness of sin had separated Father and Son that dark night. The grimness of the situation prompted the Lord to send in Moses and Elijah in what theologians describe as the transfiguration. The two came to provide courage and to remind Christ of the nature of the mission He was on – that it wouldn't be long before the *formula* for man's *salvation* was reworked

and righteousness made to pass through the
Son of God, who was about to die!

God's call is always the first manifestation that He has
poured His favor upon someone. We are not to question
His criteria because that is up to Him. I can imagine that
were He here today, in *righteous disapproval* the world would
have warned Him not to go into the slums of Kibera or
Majengo because those places are dangerous and teem
with hardcore prostitutes. We would have whispered in
His righteous ear to avoid Hollywood and Nollywood and
Bollywood celebrities because their ways are evil and they
deserve no salvation.

Indignantly, we would have doubted His very divinity for
associating with African governments run by despots, by
ministering to us through morally-wounded pastors – and
by reaching deep into the heathen lands to raise a people
called by His name.

A Call Manifests Anointing
It took me many years to understand the significance of
God's call. Later, as I looked back at the amazing journey
God had brought me through, it occurred to me that the
call I answered that Sunday morning in a Ugandan church
was *manifestation* of something that had happened in my

life right from conception. The Lord had anointed and set me apart as an earthly vessel He would use to minister to His people in Uganda, Kenya and beyond.

Anointment to leadership has been viewed by cynics as the kind of stuff for wishful thinkers, as an approach that has been used by autocrats, apologists for theocracy and groups around the world bent on showcasing themselves as superior to others – to subjugate them. In reality, the matter of anointment is a divine prerogative executed by the Creator Himself. In His deep wisdom, He has selected genealogies around the world and filled them with grace from birth. These are the individuals He has used to steer the ship of history toward a preordained outcome.

In biblical times, there were the Levites. They were used by God to speak to the Israelites by propagating laws the Lord granted to guide His people. In the *traditional* African society, there were lineages that were seen as members of a royal priesthood, people who, by virtue of birth in the bloodline of leadership, were expected to one day become *leaders* in the community. This was the case among families born into the bloodline of priesthood or born into royalty of the nature of the Buganda, Swazi or Kumasi kingdoms.

In modern times, God's anointing has been extended to any family that is willing to serve Him. He has actively reached out to communities and people groups that were once regarded as outcasts. He has invited the Indian lower castes, African-Americans of the United States, and even the lowly Bushmen of the Kalahari. The key is that as He gets into these communities, He works with those He has:

a. **Identified and set apart from conception.** As the Creator, He takes His time to configure the genetic framework of a child in the womb so that the child is freed from roots stained by demonic activities in the child's past. As the child grows, he or she may experience the burdens all humans have to bear, but the child will not be broken by them because he or she is under the care of God's grace.

b. **Given discerning eyes.** These are the favored men and women the Lord has given the rare gift of being able to read situations way before others can. They have the inspired ability to *smell* sin and avoid its path like a plague. They are the people we see around us who appear so moral till their presence alone makes others uncomfortable. What sets them apart is the inner eye God has given them to see events in the spiritual realm and act to warn others about what they see coming.

c. **Filled with faith.** This is what the Lord did with Abraham, Moses, Paul and other biblical greats. In a world that is reeling and rocking under the weight of sin, it takes only those whose faith is firmly established in the Lord to lead His people safely through the stormy waters.

Leadership as a Trust

This is where this matter gets really deep. The Lord is the only authority in heaven or on earth with the power to place *a call* to any of us because *He alone* is the leader of everything there is. He created the heavens and the earth then gave it to man to be a steward of it. In the Garden of Eden, He set our first parents – Adam and Eve – as the first set of leaders the world would ever have.

Adam and Eve were to hold the Garden of Eden in trust, as the property of God. Their minds had to remain fixated on the fact that the owner of everything created was the Lord; that He required faithfulness, honor and deep love in those who would care for His property. From that *glorious beginning,* leadership has been passed down through successive generations, right down to the present.

On the cool morning I gave my life to God and said Lord, here am I send me, I didn't know what it meant to answer *that* call. All I expected was to surrender my life and enjoy the protection of God. What I came to find out was that the call was a manifestation of the grace the Lord had extended to me as one He had anointed to carry the sword of life and cut down all the branches that stood in the way of vindication of His character of love.

Many years later, when Bishop Arthur Kitonga and I were led by the Holy Spirit to found Redeemed Gospel Church, I sensed what anointment was. It wasn't a thing that began at one's birth or even at creation in the Garden of Eden. No. Anointment was a deeper matter that went further back in history – right to the beginning. It was a matter wrapped up in who God was – in the greatness of His being. It gradually occurred to me that I was *finite* and could not understand what it meant to be anointed to lead God's people; I could only follow the LEADER of the ages as He locked my little hand in His to help me lead His people. My role was to go to the shoreline and dip my foot in His footsteps as I encouraged the flock to follow my example. Leadership was following God!

TWO
RELOCATING ROOTS

I do not know what Mahatma Gandhi saw in Christians that warranted the indicting comment he made – "I like your Christ, I do not like your Christians. Your Christians are so unlike your Christ." I may not know what made him be so scathing, but I know what he meant. He meant that as things stood then – and as they indeed are today – Christians have dived into a deeply syncretic mode and are at ease with trends that make them no different from worldly people. He saw a disconnect in the followers of Christ that troubled him, made him lament the fact that Christians were denying the world a strong moral voice that would have had a moderating influence and reassured people around the world about the future. He wanted a Christianity that remained faithful to its roots.

Many years later, as a bishop in Machakos, Kenya; not too long after I had been ordained, I contemplated the words of Gandhi and played them into my life. I was born into the family of a drunkard who lived his life to appease only himself, to cause discomfort to the weakest in the village. So troublesome was Dad in the village that on the day he died, not too many people said they would miss him. He was buried and forgotten and would only be remembered as the man who abused illicit brew till it killed him. None of the gathered mourners knew that God was rewriting the history of my broken home through the lost son of Mboko Kitonyi and Wayua, who had fled to Uganda.

In the Kenyan town of Machakos, I stood in awe on the day I arrived with my wife Gertrude to lay a foundation for the first Redeemed Gospel Church. Gertrude and I had served God in Uganda, where we got married after I persuaded her Toro kin that I was the best thing that ever happened in her life. Now blessed with children, I asked myself why God had chosen me to open the work of our church in the eastern region of Kenya.

Why the son of a despised drunkard?

It was the first time the Lord revealed to me the powerful secret of my life. Through the brokenness of my father, I had become who I was today. I was a child of the roots of a humble mother who never lived to guide her son. The blessings chosen and stored in the heavenly storehouse of grace for Dad and Mom would follow me all my life as long as I honored them as the parents who gave me life. I was a son who had germinated from the seed of suffering and humility was going to be my heritage.

Impact of Roots

I was unlucky to have had a father and mother who didn't serve the Lord. Many people are of similar misfortune. As the Lord calls us to leadership, however, He is always in the unsettling habit of having us examine our roots so He can help us confront the ugliness and hindrances of the past – to remove the intractable launching pads Satan and his demonic cohorts may use to attack us and the people the Lord has entrusted in our hand to lead. The Lord leads us to the laboratory of origins, where He *guides* us in the process of decoding our foundations so that nothing will carry forward that may compromise His mission.

This is one of the most foundational and most critical aspects of leadership since the Eden, but it is also the one Satan has completely blinded us to. The demonic world is aware that if we were to understand the depth of this matter, that world would lose a foothold in Africa – and around the world. This is because on this Dark Continent, and in many places around the world, the demonic world has weaved its agenda so intricately into the fabric of life as to make its dark agenda a way of life. Our roots, as

Africans, have therefore been established on the basis of ritualistic acts, speeches, songs, dances and all manner of attitudes inspired by the forces of darkness.

As the Lord calls one to leadership, He does not require any of us to be righteous – because we are fallen sinners and our only claim to righteousness is through Christ's sacrificial death on the cross – but He demands of us an examination of our roots so that we may delink from that past of *binding covenants* sealed with the blood of demonic sacrifices to a new dispensation that restores our heritage in the Abrahamic covenant, which was sealed by the blood of Christ on the cross. The sacrificial rituals our ancestors ushered us into in the *ithembeos* across the land have to be ostracized from our blood as Christ's cleansing blood washes us as white as cotton.

This is deep. It is at the very center of the reason many so called leaders have failed to live up to their billing and have become a burden to the people they purport to lead. Across Africa, and around the world, we have leaders who rose to the positions of leadership they occupy without having examined their lives and come to terms with their roots. They don't know whether the binding covenants members of their past families entered were sealed with the ruinous blood of demonic influences or the sacrificial and cleansing blood of Christ. This is a significant matter because the Lord warns each of us that He punishes evildoers up to the third and fourth generation.

> You shall not bow down to them or worship them; for I, the LORD your God, am a jealous God, punishing the children for the sin of the parents to the third and fourth generation of those who hate me … (Exodus 20:5, NIV).

The reason it is crucial to examine one's life before taking up leadership is because our roots and the heritage they bestow upon us will determine the kind of leadership we offer.

If the roots we bring to leadership were established in the enmeshing foundation of binding satanic rituals, the leadership offered will be one that ushers the led to be partakers of the glories of those very rituals and the powers they represent.

This is a case of carrying on in the mode of glorifying the ancient deceiver – that *treacherous* schemer whose genuine happiness is triggered only when He leads God's people to doubt the inspired narrative weaved around the covenant sealed by Christ's blood at Calvary. It is a case of affirming the power and relevance of old rituals in one's present life.

Satan's Diabolical Lies

In much the same manner Lucifer, who became known as Satan orchestrated a ferocious rebellion in heaven and presented himself as an alternative center of power in the universe, he has continued to traverse the universe with his deadly lies, claiming he owns the world and can bless those who worship him. He has positioned himself as the leader of the universe – a force capable even of hiving off a piece of earthly real estate to Christ Himself. These were his words after Christ was baptized (Revelation 12:7-12):

> [7] And there was war in heaven: Michael and his angels fought against the dragon; and the dragon fought and his angels,
>
> [8] And prevailed not; neither was their place found any more in heaven.
>
> [9] And the great dragon was cast out, that old serpent, called the Devil, and Satan, which deceiveth the whole world: he was cast out into the earth, and his angels were cast out with him.
>
> [10] And I heard a loud voice saying in heaven, Now is come salvation, and strength, and the kingdom of our God, and the power of his Christ: for the accuser of our brethren is cast down, which accused them before our God day and night.

11 And they overcame him by the blood of the Lamb, and by the word of their testimony; and they loved not their lives unto the death.

12 Therefore rejoice, ye heavens, and ye that dwell in them. Woe to the inhabiters of the earth and of the sea! for the devil is come down unto you, having great wrath, because he knoweth that he hath but a short time.

What we see here is a narrative that is at the heart of the great gift of leadership. There are two contending visions in the world – one presented to us by God as the Creator of the universe, the other presented by Satan as the rebel who seeks to continue in his ways of presenting God as a cruel, calculating and sinister deity. These two camps are embroiled in a ferocious battle to win souls. It is in this pursuit of souls that the *contending* camps enlist men and women who will lead the fight.

Satan and his demonic cohorts seek to persuade man that he is the giver of wealth, health and strength and that he alone should be worshiped. There are many who have been swayed by those lies and have kept their roots firmly established in the ritualistic shedding of blood to ratify a covenant that binds them to Satan. Christ, on the other hand, pleads that we relocate our roots from the troubled covenants and rituals of doom; that we may find our way back to the *Abrahamic heritage*, where we have been made heirs of the prince of peace, partakers in the great joys ushered in by Emmanuel, the Son of God Himself.

Roots as a Launching Pad

As I said earlier, I was unlucky to have had my roots in the *shaky foundation* of a broken home – as was established by my father and mother. In their quest to find peace in a world they couldn't control, Dad and Mom *deepened* links with cultural roots that had ruled supreme in the village and Dad topped it off by drinking like his life depended on it. They got caught up in the deep roots that gave birth to black magic and other demonic manifestations because they lacked knowledge of a different way of life.

The two contending forces are aware of the critical role our roots play as a launching pad in our lives. They are aware that the blood shed to ratify the covenants acts as a conduit through which genetic manifestations of the force one is allied with may be revealed. Through the blood of a covenant, actors in the spiritual realm are able to *determine* the heritage one is a servant to – whether the heritage of the rebellious, fallen angel or that of the victorious Christ. As that is determined, agents within the two camps will then manipulate the genetic framework of those allied to them so that they become leaders of a cause. Their roots are the secret codes used to determine their suitability to serve the force they are allied to.

In Africa, some of the roots that have proved *problematic,* because of their connection to demonic influences, have also been seen as a normal way of life.

a. **Circumcision.** In many communities across Africa, the matter of circumcision is the earliest initiation to the *demonic* world. Among the Bukusu of Kenya, it is described as a time young boys are ushered to the river in the dead of the night and their foreskin cut in the presence of a snake. The blood is used to bind them to the snake for life. That snake is the ancient serpent that showed up in the Garden of Eden to cause the fall of man. It is the same old dragon that launched war in heaven against God. A young boy, initiated into an alliance with this force, nullifies his ability to become a *godly* leader because to lead, one has to take the led to a better place.

b. **An illegitimate child.** A child born out of wedlock comes into the world with the *disadvantage* of being conceived out of honor. He or she is ushered into the world on the basis of an illicit union that acted outside the framework of God's law. This matter of illegitimacy becomes a scarlet letter the demonic world will constantly activate as a launching pad to compromise leadership in anyone. For a leader to emerge out of this wounded foundation, he or she must relocate his or her roots from the burden of illegitimacy to the *sonship* and *daughtership* of God. The Abrahamic covenant must become his or her new heritage as the old shackles of being a child born out of wedlock are replaced by the freeing power of God's legitimacy.

c. **Birth into polygamy.** Being born into a polygamous situation is another of the dangers Satan places us in early in life so that it acts as a launching pad for his attacks on us. He uses the brokenness and cold dysfunction of such a competition-ridden set up to *sow all the wrong seeds* in us – strife, fear, negativity, competition, slander and other evils. Once again, the only way a leader may emerge out of such a toxic situation is to purposefully relocate roots from the brokenness of polygamy to the cross, where Christ's cleansing blood was shed to snatch us from the jaws of traps laid by Satan at *birth*. That blood is the reason we can become effective leaders as it purifies our hearts and delivers us as blameless vessels to be used in the war to liberate *fallen man.* Christ replaces the blood of polygamy that runs in our veins with His cleansing blood!

d. **Naming.** Naming in Africa was *designed* to maintain a lineage and propel culture to future generations. Most children were named:

- After an ancestor whose stock in trade may have been a magician, a night runner or a reviled murderer. That innocent name may in the future act as a launching pad used by demonic forces to instill in the child the very character of the person they are named after. It is a root we must examine!

- After a season. Seasons are established by patterns determined in the spiritual realm. A child born during a season of harvest will inevitably be one who draws souls to Christ; one who was born during drought will kill the spirits of others – unless Christ's blood is invited to wash him or her.

There are other rituals of a demonic nature that take place at birth in Africa – like tying a talisman around the waist of a child, christening the child the names of ancestors who may have been sorcerers or black magicians and even worshiping village gods to dedicate the child to them. These are acts that bind a child to demonic forces and will compromise his or her ability to be an effective leader unless his or her roots are shifted from that background of allegiance to Satan to an allegiance to Christ.

Satan's Redefinition Rejected

Only moments after Christ was baptized and was about to start His earthly ministry, Satan showed up and attempted to redefine the nature and source of power in leadership. He tried to rearrange the deck by relocating power from the throne of God to himself. Listen to this:

> 4 Jesus, full of the Holy Spirit, left the Jordan and was led by the Spirit into the wilderness, [2] where for forty days he was tempted by the devil. He ate nothing during those days, and at the end of them he was hungry.
>
> [3] The devil said to him, "If you are the Son of God, tell this stone to become bread."
>
> [4] Jesus answered, "It is written: 'Man shall not live on bread alone.'"
>
> [5] The devil led him up to a high place and showed him in an instant all the kingdoms of the world. [6] And he said to him, "I will give you all their authority and splendor; it has been given to me, and I can give it to anyone I want to. [7] If you worship me, it will all be yours."

⁸Jesus answered, "It is written: 'Worship the Lord your God and serve him only.'"

⁹The devil led him to Jerusalem and had him stand on the highest point of the temple. "If you are the Son of God," he said, "throw yourself down from here. ¹⁰For it is written:

"'He will command his angels concerning you
    to guard you carefully;
¹¹they will lift you up in their hands,
    so that you will not strike your foot against a stone.'"

¹²Jesus answered, "It is said: 'Do not put the Lord your God to the test.'"

¹³When the devil had finished all this tempting, he left him until an opportune time" (Luke 4:1-13, KJV).

I shudder to imagine what would have happened had the Son of God succumbed to Satan's diabolical lies. It would have redefined the source of power in the universe, altered the formula for leadership in the world as power would have flowed from him to leaders rather than from God to leaders. This is a critical matter because it is at the heart of what leadership really is – then, now and into eternity.

The spirited attempt by Satan and his demonic cohorts to redefine leadership as *power flowing from Satan to human leaders* is the reason nations, churches and leading corporations are embroiled in endless turmoil. This ancient deceiver has managed to persuade great men and women that he is indeed the source of their power, strength and inspiration – that he controls the resources of the world and should be worshiped. This attempt at redefinition of leadership is responsible for the spate of leaders across Africa, and the world, who bow to Satan and lead their nations through demonic rituals. It is the reason powerful televangelists have been accused of drawing their fanatical and outsized following from the bloody rituals designed to act as a net that fishes men and locks them up in the fold of their master.

Leadership builds, inspires, saves ...

In John 10:10 (NIV), Christ speaks with force when He says The thief comes only to steal and kill and destroy; I have come that they may have life, and have it to the full. Christ, the leader of God's flock, draws a sharp contrast between what is the core character of leadership and what is the core character of pretentious lies. Leading is about building, inspiring, saving, while pretense is about stealing, killing and destroying. What Christ did was to lay it in the open that all through the ages, there has only been one LEADER and it is from Him that all power and majesty has been drawn. God is the leader, the Creator from who all His servants will derive the power and authority they need to lead His flock. The flock may be in the church, in a nation, in a corporation, in school or in any other set up where humans are to be found.

The ultimate aim of the leadership the Creator bestows on man is to share God's life in full with the led. As leaders, therefore, we stand accused whenever the nations we lead; the churches we lead; the schools we lead; the armies we lead; or the corporations we lead lack the ability to give life and give it in full – on behalf of the Creator. As we have seen, therefore, we have to relocate our roots from the compromising negative foundations we were born with to the transformative covenant of Christ, where the only source of our leadership strength is God, the Creator and Ruler of the universe.

So ... Will African Leadership Survive?

The continent is awash with leaders of nations, churches, corporations and institutions that have failed to relocate their roots from the inspiration of demonic forces to the assuredness of Christ's blood. Rather than pledge allegiance to the heritage of Abraham, they pledge allegiance to the blood of rituals founded in deceit, rebellion and pretense. The question, thus, is: can African leadership, founded on such false premises, survive? Will Africa overcome?

In the next chapter, we are going to demonstrate that the time has come for Africa not only to survive, but to thrive under a new crop of leaders who have understood the amazing power of relocated roots, men and women who have embraced the heritage of Abraham and have inherited the land promised to the father of faith.

THREE
VISIONARY LEADERSHIP

The fallen South African President, Nelson Mandela, was born in his deeply wounded nation at the height of the discredited *apartheid* system of governance. It was a system that segregated blacks and treated them worse than dogs in their own motherland. Born in the Transkei area, young Nelson watched the nation he was growing up in with much trepidation, stunned that earlier generations of his warrior community had not put up stiff resistance and pushed back the Boers who were focused on *dispossessing* the blacks and inheriting all the land they possibly could.

Mandela came of age at a time tensions were at an all-time high. The nation was bleeding from racial inequality and laws were being made to keep the nation's races apart. In high school and later, in college, he searched his soul and became aware that something was wrong with a *governance* system that deliberately separated human beings on the basis of color and not much more. He was troubled by the notion that whites were better than blacks and were to be kept away from contamination because their skin color was lighter than the black one. It was a *travesty*, he felt.

In college, therefore, when Mandela had his chance, he enrolled in Law School, where he was sure to acquire the knowledge he would one day need to legally take on the *monstrous* system that had presided over the *dehumanization* of his people. Indeed, in Law School, Mandela's sense of urgency about the state of affairs in his nation could no longer allow him to feel settled – he became restless, a man on a mission. He wanted his people to be free, to be at peace in their own land. He found segregation an obnoxious notion that had no place where human beings existed. The question was – *how was it going to be defeated?*

In his book *Long Walk to Freedom* Mandela reflected on the circumstances of his birth, his upbringing, his moments of joy and grief and his days at Law School. In his mind, he formed a vision of the nature of a nation he saw emerge in South Africa after apartheid was defeated. He envisioned a nation run on the basis of racial tolerance and justice. His was a South Africa where people felt accepted, animals felt protected, trees felt needed, and leaders felt the urge to relentlessly do the right thing. This was a *vision* Mandela said he was prepared to live for, but if need be, he was prepared to die for. The vison was clear!

Mandela came out of Law School armed with a degree he would never use much because as soon as he came out of school, it didn't take long for him to be noticed and drawn into the movement that was set on liberating the nation. The African National Congress (ANC) became the vehicle he was going to use to set his people free. Because of his activism, his daring role in organizing spectacular meetings that made powerful resolutions about the future blacks wanted, he was noticed by the authorities as well. What followed was the strongest test of will we have ever seen in modern times anywhere around the world.

He was locked up on Robben Island.

He was subjected to hard labor.

His marriage to Winnie collapsed.

His health deteriorated.

It was twenty seven years of pain for his vision.

Many years later, the world held its breath in awe as a frail Nelson Mandela walked out to freedom. In jail, the man had become a revered leader because of the power of his vision. He had emerged the fulcrum of all the forces bent of ridding the troubled nation of *laws* and *structures* steeped in oppression. His first act, when he became President, was to institute a Truth and Justice Commission, where all South Africans would come together to confess and seek forgiveness for past misdeeds and crimes. It turned out to be one of the most powerful tools ever used in Africa to put ghosts of the past behind so that a common front could emerge. It was all in keeping with his vision.

Key Elements in Visionary Leadership

I have told the inspiring story of Mandela to highlight key elements in visionary leadership.

a. **A visionary leader is born.** In most *leadership* books today, you will notice that authors believe a leader can be molded, trained and caused to be great. I'm not here to debate that line of thought. I'm here to explain that *visionary leadership is a natural occurrence*. It happens only among those the Lord has anointed and wired with the right genetic disposition to one day undertake a particular task for which He has called them. By their anointing, they have been preordained to act in ways that will confound man as they move to fulfill that role for which the Lord has placed them in the world at that time. This is the reason Scripture says this of leaders:

- Romans 13:1 – Let everyone be subject to the governing authorities, for there is no authority except that which God has established. The authorities that exist have been established by God (NIV).

- Judges 2:16 – From time to time, the Lord would choose special leaders known as judges. These judges would lead the Israelites into battle and defeat the enemies that made raids on them (CEV).

The Lord does not wait until a child is born, grown and chosen a career path before intercepting him or her for leadership; by the time He calls, He only makes manifest to man what He had already done before conception – anointed a leader and wired him or her for a specific assignment on earth.

b. **A visionary leader has the inner eye or *discernment*.** He or she is able to see the world around through the eyes of the Creator. He has been given that rare gift of stepping away from the prevailing realities of our time to see it through eyes that will fashion a Spirit-led solution – all to God's glory. The inner eye is what gives leaders the ability to connect with God's desire on a *minute-by-minute* basis. It makes a leader an instrument of God, a man or woman chosen to carry out the edicts of heaven here on earth. It is much like being an ambassador, a representative of God in these realms below. It takes that inner eye to see the world through the eyes of its Creator.

c. **A visionary leader is in tune with God's will.** This is the leader who wakes up each morning on bended knees to seek the will of God in his or her life. It is the leader who goes through the day *listening* keenly to what the Lord has to say; watching keenly what the Lord is showing; feeling and touching his or her way through *everything* because of the *awareness* that he or she has been called to minister to God's hurting, broken children. The Lord has equipped this leader with rare gifts:

- A sound mind. The mind of such a leader is an earthly extension of the mind of God. Through it, the Lord makes crucial *decisions* designed to create an atmosphere where His people may safely worship Him. David was a man the Lord testified about saying: *After removing Saul, he made David their king. God testified concerning him: 'I have found David son of Jesse, a man after my own heart; he will do everything I want him to do* (Acts 13:22, NIV). A leader of sound mind will remain connected to God and will act only after hearing the still voice of God.

- A heart of love. The word *care* may replace *love* in this context. This is a leader who feels the pain of the lowly, the downtrodden, the weak and the suffering. His or her heart is filled with deep pain when people are sick, hungry, oppressed, broken or hopeless. This was the case when Christ saw people: *When he saw the crowds, he had compassion on them, because they were harassed and helpless, like sheep without a shepherd* (Matthew 9:36, NIV). An anointed leader will feel the heartbreak with pity when people suffer – he or she will move with swiftness to restore comfort.

- Grace or favor. This is a leader for whom the endless storehouse of heavenly blessings is constantly open, a man or woman the Lord acts on each prayer he or she offers and covers him or her under the wings of His *loving grace*. The people a leader of such a nature leads find favor with God on account of the faithfulness of their leader.

They find blessings in good health, strength, food, shelter and wealth because the will of their leader is the will of God.

d. **A visionary leader prepares future leaders.** He or she, in partnership with God, will act to identify the next crop of leaders. The *legacy* he or she leaves behind is one that will be protected by successors who understand the stakes and the vision that has brought the people thus far. Nations and kingdoms perish when leadership is transferred from men and women of vision to those who neither have anointment nor have been called to lead. To the extent that a visionary leader can, he or she must ensure that a smooth transition of power to a man or woman of anointing is enabled.

Leadership Inspired by Demons

In an earlier chapter, we discussed the contending forces in the universe. We mentioned the fact that all power is derived from the Lord, the one who created the heavens and the earth. We also *mentioned* the fact that after Satan's rebellion, that ancient deceiver set up an alternative power structure to compete that of God. As things stand today, we live under the dominion of systems and structures controlled by demonic forces in most nations on earth.

Satan and his demonic agents have worked feverishly to place men and women in power – people whose allegiance is to the principalities and rulers of darkness.

These are the leaders who presided over broken nations characterized by enormous bloodshed across Africa and in many nations around the world. Their leadership has been a painful harvest in the blood of God's children as they have instigated civil wars, plundered national treasure and acted in ways approved by the bloodthirsty hounds in the world of demonic ritualization. Examples abound:

a. **In Uganda,** there ruled a man who stormed into the State House through the barrel of a gun. Idi Amin Dada was so ruthless that during his reign many Ugandan professionals lost their lives, many Christians were killed, many fled the nation and the economy eventually collapsed.

b. **In Rwanda,** the demonic world instigated vicious tribal hate between the Tutsi and the Hutu, which later led to one of the worst bloodlettings in the world – in the twentieth century. By the time the guns went silent, more than a million people lay dead in the heart of Africa.

c. **In Angola,** the endless civil war that pitted forces allied to Jonas Savimbi against forces allied to the

Head of State, Eduardo Dos Santos, reduced the nation to rubble as thousands of innocent civilians lost their lives.

Satan and his agents are on the prowl and have partnered with men and women who lack anointing to generate the blood needed for sacrifices in the underworld. They have become true to the Lord's warning that they come to kill, destroy and steal. They have presided over a continent that has witnessed mass starvation, endless civil wars, the onset of pandemics like the dreaded Ebola and HIV-AIDS, assassinations, looting of state coffers, destruction of the environment and ineptness in policy execution.

I need to point out that Africa's painful past is a direct product of the continent's love affair with leaders whose allegiance is not to the Creator. They act for darkness. Lead under the inspiration of darkness. And *instigate* wars to fill the blood banks of hell with blood for sacrifices to their master. These are the leaders in whose nations roads have become highways of death, hospitals have become institutions of tears, and disciplined forces have become men and women deployed to steal, destroy and kill.

Africa thus suffers cursed leadership because we have failed to move our people from the realm controlled by

Satan and his agents to one inspired by Christ. We have suffered lack of God's favor because the leaders we have are not men and women the Lord anointed to lead His people – they are men and women who *anointed themselves, called themselves* and *arrogated to themselves* power to decide what is good for a helpless people.

They have become a curse!

Therefore, when Scripture makes mention of leaders as agents appointed by God, it does not include those who draw their inspiration from Satan. It does not regard them as leaders because they lack God's anointing. They are only leaders in the parallel structure created by rebellion, where their diabolical master has caused them to believe he has power to share with them.

There's an Answer to Africa's Leadership Woes

The despair felt across Africa has reached the ears of the Lord. The Lord is about to raise a new generation of leaders who will wipe away the gains made by the demonic world as Christ's reign of righteousness takes root. As a keen observer of events in Africa, I was touched when I read in an authoritative magazine that the continent's prospects for emergence as a leading investment hub and key economic player have never been better. It based its uplifting prognostications on the continent's embrace of democratic tenets.

a. **A free press.** This is a thriving, robust press that has the ability to carry out *investigative* journalism, report stories without fear or favor, and write editorials geared toward holding leaders to account. Across Africa, this is a tenet taking root as leaders feel the heat of demand for credible governance.

b. **An independent judiciary.** This is a judiciary that bases its judgments and findings on nothing but the power of evidence. It does not sink to the manipulative tune of the executive or the military junta in leadership at the time. It seldom relies on circumstantial evidence and is seen to be manned by officials of the highest integrity.

c. **An *assertive* legislature.** This is the wing of *government* tasked to make laws for the nation. Across Africa, this branch of governance has been used as a stamp for bad laws originated by the Head of State to frustrate the Opposition and perceived enemies of the state. It has been used to uphold unpopular laws left in the books long after oppressive colonial masters who formulated them departed. Africa cries out for an assertive legislature composed of men and women of high integrity, leaders whose only agenda is to make life better for the people.

It wasn't too long after the magazine's story that President Barack Obama flew to Nairobi, Kenya, to open the much-anticipated Global Entrepreneurship Summit, a gathering that brought together top leaders of the world's largest companies. In his keynote address, the President of the United States lauded progress made on the continent in the pivotal areas of democratic governance, tolerance of divergent opinions, opening up of space for women to play a greater role in leadership, and fostering a conducive environment for investment.

In that inspiring speech at the UNEP headquarters, in Gigiri, and the magazine's warm endorsement of Africa, what I saw was evidence that God was moving to take control of the narrative in Africa. He was establishing a foundational framework He was going to use to wrestle Africa from the hands of satanic leaders who have shed too much blood and denied His people space to worship. He was extending the deep roots of the Righteous Branch, the great Emmanuel, from the plains of Judah to the troubled plains and mountains and valleys of Africa.

> "The days are coming," declares the LORD, "when I will raise up for David a righteous Branch, a King who will reign wisely and do what is just and right in the land" (Jeremiah 23:5).

Yes, there is an answer to Africa's inept leadership. It is in visionary leadership. It is in leadership founded on the deep roots of Davidic anointing. It is servant-leadership built on the premise that there has and there always will be only one leader – GOD. Those to whom He has extended the divine call to be partakers in His mighty act of shaping the destiny of the world are called leaders only in so far as they remain loyal to divine guidance and the *rich heritage* of men and women of vision.

FOUR
GRACE UNDER FIRE

David couldn't have been older than twenty five when he first went to the sprawling grazing fields to visit with his older brothers. His brothers had been gone from home for a while to find greener pastures for the sheep of their father Jesse. When the young David got to the place his brothers were, he met a scene he hadn't anticipated and could have never been prepared for. A Philistine giant called Goliath had just arrived like he had done over the last couple of evenings and was taunting the Israelites by urging them to identify one general to fight him instead of engaging whole armies in a ruinous war.

The generals in Israel were scared stiff of the giant. None of them volunteered to take on the towering man, who for forty days had come out to mock the Israelites and the God they *worshiped*. In those days of theocratic governance among the Israelites, the perception was established that by mocking the God of Israel, Philistine was showcasing itself as having a superior God.

David ran into this dangerous and scandalous situation at a time he couldn't have imagined himself any better than the *seasoned* fighters in the nation's army. He most certainly couldn't have been stronger than the frontline generals who had taken on foes of the past and defeated them. This explains the consternation David had to endure as he listened to the blasphemous words that dropped off the lips of the massive man. Why couldn't any of the generals take on Goliath? Why couldn't his brothers do it?

Amazed by what he was witnessing, David pulled one of his brothers aside and asked who the man was.

"Goliath is the name. He is a Philistine general," David's brother said, afraid to even mention the giant's name.

"Why can't somebody take on him?" David asked. "He is blaspheming the name of our God!"

David's brother read him right – the words were part consternation part accusation. Why are you letting the name of our God be dragged in the mud by this heathen? Ashamed by David's words, he urged the boy to go back home and relay the information that all was well in the field. As David made his way, though, he was even more troubled by what he had witnessed. His fears grew even stronger when he told his father Jesse about what he had seen and the old man appeared troubled.

On David's next visit, he was shocked to see that the madness he'd witnessed on the first visit was still ongoing. This time, though, as soon as he relayed greetings from Dad and gave them the food items he had brought them, he asked to see the generals.

"Why?" his older brother asked sternly.

"I will fight Goliath," he said.

As they laughed, he walked away to find the generals. It didn't take long before he got them persuaded that he wasn't mad; that he wasn't delusional. He was just an ordinary young Israelite who had grown up being told that YAHW was an all-powerful God who was able fight His wars through faithful vessels like David. David was going to make himself available to be used by God if others lacked faith in God's ability to vindicate Himself.

The generals gave David armor and the military fatigue he would need in war against the giant.

David declined.

He prepared a sling.

And five stones.

It was a sight to behold as the young son of Jesse made his way to the battlefield. He was armed with a couple of items Goliath and those assembled to watch his *foolishness* unfold could see: a sling, a bag of stones and obvious haughtiness. What they couldn't see was the weapon that was the most potent of all. It was his faith in God. Faith gave him the courage to face the giant, to envision victory and to dedicate that victory to God before he even had it bagged. He was certain of the outcome because he knew the God his father Jesse had told him about.

At a safe distance, David finally stopped and heard the *blasphemous* words repeated one more time by the giant. He also heard the mockery Goliath directed at him because of his youth, inexperience and foolishness. Indeed, he heard the vicious words directed at the cowardly Israel generals who chose to *sacrifice* a young lad instead of offer *themselves* to fight a man's fight.

In my mind's eye, I can see David's bewildered brothers discuss the matter in low tones. What were they going to tell their father about David's death? How would they break the news of the boy's death at the hands of a heathen general who was supposed to fight fellow soldiers and not a young man whose only role had been to supply food and water to them in the grazing fields. Who was going to handle the public relations of this mess?

David said a prayer, then trapped his first stone in the sling. He then warned the Philistine general that while he came with a sword and great armor, David came with *faith* in the God of Israel. It was the first time he had revealed the armor no one could see. Goliath must have wondered what faith was and what it had to do with this fight. To him, this was about strength, size, vigor. He was three or four times bigger than David and was sure to destroy the boy in seconds. The fight was over as soon as it started, he thought, as he made his way toward David.

In that hour of need, David got the sling spinning in the air as he took aim and let the stone fly. Before Goliath could take any further steps toward him, the stone crashed into his massive head with force, finding the very spot the Lord wanted it to hit. In that divine moment, the generals of Israel and the gathered Philistines watched as Goliath's huge body hit the ground and didn't require a doctor to pronounce him dead because everybody could tell – in that split second – that it wasn't David who had slayed Goliath; it was God. The sling was just a medium.

David ran and cut the neck of the fallen Philistine general to bring it back to Israel as testimony to what the Lord could do. It was a grisly trophy to bring home, but it had to be so. There were moments when victory required the display of trophies people least expected.

Attributes of Courage

David's is a *powerful* story of courage. It is a demonstration of what leadership is about when one is anointed by God to play a role in the great plot of redemption. *Grace under fire* is a fancy way of saying *courageous*. The Lord needs men and women of courage in this broken world to confront the devastating situations caused by evil forces. He has implanted key attributes in them because He is aware that bloodshed, hunger, earthquakes and civil wars are not matters to be handled without these attributes.

    a. Faith. Abraham has been called the father of faith, the patriarch whose acts of leaving his ancestral land and willingness to sacrifice his son Isaac were counted as evidence of deep and abiding faith in God. Throughout history, the world has witnessed similar display of faith in great leaders like Mother

Teresa, Nelson Mandela and Mahatma Gandhi. These were leaders who had faith in the power of the vision they espoused. They acted on the basis of birthing the vision, giving credibility to its saving power and tying its glory to divine origination. Does this mean leaders have to be Christians to be effective? Not at all. But leaders have to have faith in the Supreme Being credited with creation and the splendor we witness in the galaxies, the great mountain ranges and oceanic water masses of the world. That Supreme Being makes natural systems work in coordinated harmony and is the reason the laws of nature direct biological clocks to activate when a mating season comes, leaves to turn golden with *beauty* when autumn approaches, and summer to shower the brilliant rays of the sun rather than the snowflakes of the winter days. It is faith in this deity that makes leaders great!

b. Vision. In the last chapter, we discussed the role of vision in shaping great leadership. For a leader to be courageous, he or she has to be guided by the star of vision. There has to be a strong belief in the vision's capacity to transform lives and to create an atmosphere conducive for worship to take place. Vision, thus, is the *ingredient* needed to give courage the potency it requires. It is the element that causes all other elements in leadership to gel – because it has the glue necessary for courage to emerge.

c. **Endurance.** We live in a troubled world overridden by wars, famine, earthquakes and civil wars – as we have already established. It is a place inhabited by forces of doom whose only desire is to *wreak* havoc and blame it on God. In this scheme of things, the Lord has wired those He has anointed to lead with that extra ounce of *endurance* they need to *withstand* fear when they see devastation in nations, churches and companies around them. *Endurance* is the force a great leader relies on to lead his or her people through troubled times; the ray of hope that glitters in the darkness of horrific tunnels and offers that one last push to hold on.

Scripture on Courage

There are certain traditions that hold the belief that when Satan was ejected from heaven, he went around the universe to find a place he could be accepted. All the other worlds *rejected* him, not ready to welcome a *destructive* liar who had openly competed God. He later came to our earth, where our first parents, Adam and Eve, welcomed him. These are some of those mythical stories we are unable to verify, but it points to the fact that Satan came to our backyard and has perfected the art of *killing, stealing* and *destroying* everything in his way.

Aware that His people would suffer under the cruelty of Satan's schemes, God inspired the men and women who wrote the Bible to sprinkle strategic verses on courage in the pages of the *holy book*. He wanted His people, through the ages, to face the cruelty demonic agents would direct at them with courage and determination to overcome. These inspired verses have been relevant since the days of John the Revelator and Emperor Domitian, the troubled days of Martin Luther and the painful days of Joan of Arc. It appears, though, as if the verses were written for a time such as we are in. Leaders today will do well to read the words of the Lord as were pronounced by His servants:

- **1 Chronicles 28:20 (KJV)** - And David said to Solomon his son, Be strong and of good courage, and do [it]: fear not, nor be dismayed: for the LORD God, [even] my God, [will be] with thee; he will not fail thee, nor forsake thee, until thou hast finished all the work for the service of the house of the LORD.
- **1 Corinthians 10:13 (KJV)** - There hath no temptation taken you but such as is common to man: but God [is] faithful, who will not suffer you to be tempted above

that ye are able; but will with the temptation also make a way to escape, that ye may be able to bear [it].

- **Joshua 1:9 (KJV)** - Have not I commanded thee? Be strong and of a good courage; be not afraid, neither be thou dismayed: for the LORD thy God [is] with thee whithersoever thou goest.

- **Deuteronomy 31:6 (KJV)** - Be strong and of a good courage, fear not, nor be afraid of them: for the LORD thy God, he [it is] that doth go with thee; he will not fail thee, nor forsake thee.

- **Philippians 1:28 (KJV)** - And in nothing terrified by your adversaries: which is to them an evident token of perdition, but to you of salvation, and that of God.

Through the Apostle Paul, speaking to the Ephesians, the Lord revealed who the tormentor of His people is. In one of the most gripping narratives of Scripture, He warns about the need to guard ourselves as His followers – but more especially as leaders in the movement of destiny. The words may be seen as a warning, but I choose to see them as the wise counsel of a friend, the loving shielding of a seasoned general who is aware of incoming fire and is eager to keep his troops safe. Listen to this:

> Finally, be strong in the Lord and in his mighty power. [11] Put on the full armor of God, so that you can

take your stand against the devil's schemes. [12] For our struggle is not against flesh and blood, but against the rulers, against the authorities, against the powers of this dark world and against the spiritual forces of evil in the heavenly realms. [13] Therefore put on the full armor of God, so that when the day of evil comes, you may be able to stand your ground, and after you have done everything, to stand. [14] Stand firm then, with the belt of truth buckled around your waist, with the breastplate of righteousness in place, [15] and with your feet fitted with the readiness that comes from the gospel of peace. [16] In addition to all this, take up the shield of faith, with which you can extinguish all the flaming arrows of the evil one. [17] Take the helmet of salvation and the sword of the Spirit, which is the word of God.

[18] And pray in the Spirit on all occasions with all kinds of prayers and requests. With this in mind, be alert and always keep on praying for all the Lord's people (Ephesians 6:10-18, NIV).

Courage of Doom in the Motherland

There was once a leader in Liberia called Charles Taylor. The man orchestrated some of the worst killings Africa has ever witnessed. In an effort to show himself *courageous,* he presided over the killing of women, the plunder of a nation's meager resources, the maiming of elderly people, and raping of girls by his ruthless militia. After he was deposed, he staged a ruinous guerrilla war that finished off whatever little was left of his nation. Today the man is locked up in jail so that his influence may never again be felt on the nation he tortured.

In Uganda, Idi Amin Dada led his State Research Bureau in a campaign of terror that was designed to show him as a courageous leader who entertained no opposition. He killed opponents, killed church leaders and ruined the nation's economy with his ruthless policies of aggressively targeting hostile voices. Today the Mad Man of Uganda is buried in the desert lands of Saudi Arabia, where he fled as the Tanzania Defense Forces moved in to take over the capital city, Kampala.

We have since witnessed the ruthless regimes of African despots, men whose hands are stained with the blood of innocent Africans. They killed so many defenseless people to prove how courageous they were, but in the end hid in caves and resorted to tactics that revealed more fear than courage. If courage was about leaving home and going to the end of a railway line in a distant land, like I once did, they were going to have nothing to do with it.

The point is this – courage in Africa has always been seen as the macho acts of a dictator to protect the ill-gotten gains of his family, cronies and tribe. It has been perceived as the degree of ruthlessness deployed in defeating the voices of dissension, and the fabulousness of wealth acquired as one is resident in the State House. What most despots don't understand is that courage is measured not against terror directed at poor and hungry people, but in the heroic acts of beating back the determined onslaught of real and evident enemies.

The enemies Africa's anointed leaders of the future will have to fight will include:

a. **Poverty.** It takes enormous courage to tackle this great enemy of Africa. A leader whose desire is to fight this destructive force will have to work closely with global organizations like:

- United Nations, so that its *constituent* bodies like World Health Organization, UNICEF and UNEP may deploy their resources in a targeted campaign of poverty reduction in Africa. For a world that revels in the glories of the twenty-first century, there is no *excuse* for Africa's leaders to fail the test of leading prospering nations.

- African Union, so that a coordinated policy position may be adopted toward eradication of poverty on the continent. To the extent that Africa remains trapped in the tentacles of hunger, lack and disease, we have to attribute it to *lack of imagination* and poverty of ideas on the part of leaders.

- World Bank and IMF, so that these twin Bretton Woods institutions may become allies in the war to tame and defeat poverty. By reducing lending rates and providing grants aimed at job creation, the search for prosperity in Africa may be boosted and the menace of poverty may gradually become a problem whose end is in sight.

b. Disease. In spite of tremendous gains on the war on *diseases*, Africa remains one of the few *continents* where infant mortality, geriatric care and increasing forms of medical conditions are still problematic. It will take courageous leadership to face this great enemy and defeat it. Diseases like typhoid, cholera, Ebola, HIV-AIDS and Malaria should be defeated and declared over. It takes courage, imagination and focus – the kind of leadership only an anointed servant of the Lord can offer.

c. **Illiteracy.** This old enemy remains hold up in rural enclaves across the continent. It has kept elderly Africans from accessing services because they can't read; and has kept the rural young from preparing for a productive future because they lack fees and other requirements to be enrolled in school. The move to make *early schooling* compulsory in nations on the continent is laudable, but it lacks focus. It subjects poor children to schools of lesser quality than those whose parents can afford private and better equipped schools. The anointed leader will move in to create a level playing field in education so that all the children of a nation will have the same opportunities to learn.

d. **Security.** Unlike the past, nations in Africa have enjoyed relative peace due to lack of civil wars, but security remains compromised because of poverty, hunger and lawlessness in most cities and rural areas. War on insecurity is the final and most bitter one anointed leaders in Africa will deal with. It will end the reign of terror and fear Africans have lived with since the days of the clamor for *independence.*

> Its defeat will be the beginning of real freedom in
> Africa – the end of the dark ages.

Leadership requires courage on a scale only the Creator can offer. The Lord is gracious enough to wire His *anointed* vessels on earth with divine genetic mapping to fire up courage of the kind He built into Daniel ahead of his being hurled into a den of lions, into the three Jewish boys before being cast into a fiery furnace, into Esther before she risked her life by appearing before the king, into Moses before he stormed into Pharaoh's palace with a stern message, and into Ruth before she told Boaz that "Your people shall be my people and your God my God."

The grave challenges Africa faces need men and women of courage in the church, in politics, in the corporate sector and in the military. The motherland needs editors and reporters of valor. The days of the cowards who will steal, kill and destroy are numbered, because the Lord has commenced the act of cleansing Africa and turning her over to the groom – the leaders who will rule on the basis of the Ten Commandments and will usher God's people to a place of worship, a place of eternal rest.

FIVE
TIME

The day was finally drawing to a close. The length of our shadows had stretched behind all the mourners as Mama's casket was lowered to the ground by men and women of valor in our village. Her death had come slowly because of her prolonged illness, but when it eventually shut down all her systems and she bowed to its relentless cruelty, I had to wonder about the limited time Mama had been with us. In life, she had taken the best care of me in our poverty and had ensured our broken home felt like a home. She had given the home a sense of stability.

Mother was a diminutive Kamba woman who was *dutifully* kind and joyfully welcoming. Though she died while I was still young, she remained an inspiring force in my life. As she was eulogized and mourners said great things about her, I had to look back at the life she led. I had to think of the days she went out into the dry garden and brought back vegetables enough for just one meal. I had to recall the many nights she placed her hand on my head and assured me that her love was unfailing. I had to blink back tears when I remembered the day she walked home and said she didn't feel too well.

Now Mama lay dead.

Trapped in a coffin.

Was being lowered into another trap.

Six feet under.

Death!

After Mama was buried, I went on with life, aware death had robbed me of the only strong pillar in my life. I knew Dad was around and would be there – somewhere in my life in his drunken nature – but there was that great sense of loss I feared would not heal soon. I realized that Mama had closed a chapter in my young life, parted with the little security I had, and had ushered me into realms unknown.

Seeing mourners walk away from her fresh grave – after her burial, as the sun dipped behind the clouds yonder – I was gripped with fear. I feared for the state of our home. What were we going to do without Mama?

Mama's death, however, did not cause me to ask all the critical questions I should have. After all, I was just but a child. When Dad later died, however, I was older and had to face the *prospect* of being in the world as an orphan – a prospect that scared me even though I had *essentially* been alone for long. And though I later went on to become an astute businessman, I could not shake off the meaning of the two deaths. Why did Mama die before Dad? Was there anything a young boy could have done to extend the life of his mother on earth – even by a month or two?

In my ministry, now spanning decades, I have officiated at several funeral services and burial ceremonies and know that people ask these questions – especially of an untimely death. The truth of the matter is: *there is never an untimely death;* the only death there is … is a death whose time has come.

It's all about time!

The passing of my mother and father made me reflect on the meaning of life on earth. It made me dig deep into the reason some people die at infancy, others in adolescence, many in the middle ages, and a majority in the old age. As a leader – one anointed to serve God's people – how was I supposed to relate with time, given that I already knew man's time on earth was limited?

God Sanctified Time

I already gave a heads-up that we are dealing with matters of leadership from a point of view you won't interact with in any of the books already published on the subject. In this discussion, the intention is to get into the deeper matters of leadership so that we completely redefine how God's people will be led by politicians, pastors, bishops, chairmen of state and private corporations, and even by policymakers at the highest echelons of global bodies like the United Nations, World Bank and the International Monetary Fund. This is the reason we are about to delve into an incisive investigation of what God meant by giving anointed leaders *time* to lead His people.

The place to begin is in the beginning. In Genesis chapter 1:1-4 (NIV), the first few seconds on earth are recorded thus:

> In the beginning God created the heavens and the earth. [2]Now the earth was formless and empty, darkness was over the surface of the deep, and the Spirit of God was hovering over the waters.
> [3]And God said, "Let there be light," and there was light. [4]God saw that the light was good, and he separated the light from the darkness. [5]God called the light "day," and the darkness he called "night." And there was evening, and there was morning—the first day.

The foundational book of origins, known as Genesis, lays bare the moment it all began. It takes us back to the very first second of time on earth, makes us interact with the elements that existed when *time* and *man* left the hands of the Creator. By so doing, the writer of Genesis is revealing something deep about these two items.

a. **Time.** In the strictest sense of it, we are compelled to conclude that time was the very first item God created. He had to create time so that within it, He would place everything else He was going to create. Because nothing else had been created, however, time meant nothing as it existed within the realm of eternity – as a force that connected space from one end to the other. Aware of the role time would play once other creative works came into being, God touched time and set it loose so that it would guide the evolvement of *seasons*. He thus sanctified time by touching it with divine hands.

b. **Man.** The term man, in this context, applies to the male and female species. Man came along on the last day of creation – being the sixth day. All other animals, plants, and fishes had already been spoken into existence. On the sixth day, however, the Lord caused deep sleep to come over Adam. As he slept, the first ever surgical operation was performed as his rib was retrieved to form Eve. By *directly touching* man at creation, the Lord sanctified the life of man and it became the second item, after time, to have left the hands of God directly as it came into being.

The significance of the sanctity of man's *life* and *time* are deep matters tied to the very reason God created man. He placed man on earth so that by being in the *glorious* Garden of Eden, man would worship in peace and love. Time was to be spent in activities that brought glory and honor to God as the Garden of Eden became an *outpost* of heaven, an earthly high commission of God's heavenly abode. The Eden was to become a vibrant embassy where time was spent in activities that reflected the state of heaven on a minute-by-minute basis – in real time.

It was this divine matter of time – the way it is to be spent in worship – that Christ had on His mind when He taught His disciples how to pray. When you pray, He told them, do it this way (Luke 11:2-4, KJV):

> And he said unto them, When ye pray, say, Our Father which art in heaven, Hallowed be thy name. Thy kingdom come. Thy will be done, as in heaven, so in earth.
>
> [3] Give us day by day our daily bread.

> ⁴ And forgive us our sins; for we also forgive every one
> that is indebted to us. And lead us not into temptation;
> but deliver us from evil.

The words of interest are tucked at the tail-end of verse two: *Thy will be done, as in heaven, so in earth.* More familiar translations have it thus: *Thy will be done on earth as it is in heaven.* Christ was taking His weary disciples back to the beginning of time, when the Garden of Eden was a place of deep worship and God's glory shone through it. It was a garden of exotic beauty, where the two items sanctified by God at creation – time and man – came together to praise the Creator of the universe.

The reason we have to begin the discussion on time with the fact that time was sanctified by God is because we have to feel the impact of time on leadership. The men and women the Lord has anointed to lead have to be aware of the fact that He touched time with His own hands and gave it as a gift to those who would be placed in the role of leading worship on earth.

It gets deeper!

Ongoing Worship on Earth

That there ought to be ongoing worship on earth is the reason God anoints leaders for His children. In whatever sphere of life, He *appoints* men and women who are to lead in worship much like Lucifer led in heaven. Whenever I discuss this matter at certain forums, attendees ask what worship has to do with corporate leadership or political gamesmanship or military war planning. They wonder why I have to make secular leadership become a matter so deeply couched in the language divinity.

In an earlier chapter, we already alluded to the fact that all leadership – the power in it – is founded in the person of the Creator of the universe. It is invested in the One who owns everything there is. Because of that, whatever we do in the world is an activity that should bring glory and honor to the Creator. Each activity we engage in should be one that is an act of worship. Whether we are janitors, mid-level managers, businessmen and women or in the military, we are to carry out our duties with the sense that we are acting inside the framework of time given to us for a purpose – a purpose that will one day come to an end.

There are, of course, philosophers and scholars who seek to divorce matters secular from matters spiritual. They are more *comfortable* in a world where God is tucked neatly to the one side and earthly matters to the other. These are the philosophers and scholars who have inspired political leaders in Africa to warn religious leaders against making *pronouncements* on matters political. The failure of our time, and times past, is that we never saw through this trick of the demonic world. We failed to realize that by accepting the notion that God's agenda didn't fit in the broader schemes of life, we were taking God out of State House, Corporate Headquarters, the barracks, the marketplace and at all universities around the world. We were making a spirited attempt to deny the Creator His omnipotence, His omnipresence and omniscience.

We were trying to reduce God!

The plan of the demonic agents was to confine God to a corner of the mind of man so that time was divided up into slots where there was God's time, Me time, State time, Work time and other times. Given the nature of a work week, it did not take rocket science to realize that God's time would thus be confined to church hour and worship would all but end on earth – except for a couple of hours in a seven-day week. Satan and his agents were going to preoccupy man with a lot of activities that would draw man away from worshiping the Creator.

If you ask me whether the demonic plan succeeded, I would throw a question back at you. The question would be this: how much time do you spend in worship today? If your answer is not twenty four hours a day, you've got a problem. It is God's desire that in whatever we do, we should worship Him. As the head of a corporation, we have to create time for employees to worship, as the head of a military, we have to curve out time for the soldiers to connect with their Creator, as the head of a nation, we have to establish channels through which God's people will experience an atmosphere of endless worship.

The term *secular* was, undoubtedly, invented by forces who were out to deny the pervasive influence worship was to have on earth. These were forces bent on making it appear *cool* to say there were moments for God and moments for other things. In the moments for other things, man was not to be held accountable by God. If one went to a dirty dance party, plotted the murder of a rival, engaged in corrupt dealings or sought the services of a homosexual companion, it wasn't for God to worry at all – because that wasn't His time. It was Me time!

Anointed leadership is about calling God's people back to the inspiring script written at creation. It is about warning the people of God about how far we have veered from the plan He had for man. It is about explaining to man the connectedness of the time we live in to the time of the beginning and the time of the end – that we live *somewhere* in the middle of the gift God gave man on the day He created time and set all creation to act within it.

Connectedness of Time

The Kenyan country music singer, Roger Whitaker, *decried* the destructive impact of man on the environment in his hit song *Do I Trust You Man*. The lyrics are mournful and urgent as he urges man to up the game in saving the wild animals, taking care of the trees and building a better world for future generations. Since the world began, he says, man is about war, destruction, fear and lack of grace. In the music world, as in other realms, this is one of the few artists to have put a finger on the connectedness of time – on the fact that since time left the hands of the Creator, there has been *contiguity* in the minute-by-minute and second-by-second manner time has evolved.

The very minute I write this book *now* is connected to that first minute time left the hand of the Creator. It goes way back in relatedness to the first second of the earth's existence, to the heart of origination of the space we today occupy as the earth. Here is what this means:

   a. **Each moment of life we have is connected to the very first second and minute the Lord created the earth.** The air we breathe has changed, the foods we ate have been genetically modified by the acts of science, and the innocence of our minds has been blown asunder by breathtaking technological feats, astronomical discoveries and confounding medical breakthroughs. The only element that has remained untainted by the passage of time is time. It remains pure and fresh just like it left the hands of the Creator. It is the only gift we have that we are to individually decide how we spend each day and that decision *determines* whether we will spend the day in *worship* or in the *pursuit* of personal glory.

b. **Man came along and felt the *need* to divide up time into blocks he could comprehend.** In observance of the day and night cycles, which the Lord had set to roll on uninterrupted by any force on earth, man invented units within that cycle and called it hours. Those hours were further divided into minutes and minutes into seconds. As knowledge increased and man noted the broader blocks of time, the need arose to name those stretches of time.

- A month became the block of every thirty days, which was tagged to the nature of the journey of the moon across the sky.
- Each block of three months was lumped together and given the name a quarter. This

was designed to tie in with the fact that a year had four blocks of three months.

- Twelve of those months we strung together and given the name a year. Later, the need for even broader categorizations gave man the block of ten years known as a decade, the block of one hundred years known as a century, and the block of *one thousand* years known as a millennium.

c. **In certain cooler regions of the world, there arose the need to name time according to *prevailing weather circumstances*.** The term season was thus birthed to ascribe the names *summer* to the hot season, *winter* to the cold season, *spring* to the warming season and *autumn* to the cooling season.

d. **Just when man thought time had been named in units and reduced to an *entity* that could be defined, historians and philosophers noted characteristics that played within very broad slots of time.** These were *times* that could only be defined *way after history had happened* and patterns had clearly emerged that defined the period as different from others. The name ascribed to this time was *epoch* or *era*. This is the reason we hear of the era of dinosaurs or the epoch of the crusades.

I have no doubt that philosophers of the past felt the impact of the connectedness of time. They felt the way the times they lived in connected second-by-second to the very first second God created time. I can also imagine that sailors and students of space are keen to the *connectedness* of time. In the galaxies and other majestic starry formations, they see galactic systems that have been untainted by the adventures of man. The Andromeda and the Milky Way and other systems like Orion the Hunter point to the fact that time was not supposed to alter the fundamental nature of creation; it was supposed to affirm its genius.

The years and seasons and fascinating epochs of the past are all intimately connected to the present and each tick tock tick tock of the second hand on the clock reveals the need for man to remain primitive in the desire to see time as a divine gift – handed to us so that we may use it in the glory of God. Indeed, it speaks to the way we have spent our time on earth that all creation we have touched has come undone. We have destroyed animals and rendered certain species *extinct*; we have attacked the great wilds and caused the beautiful wildernesses to *disappear*; we have engaged in free-style industrialization and caused the globe to warm, with carbon emissions threatening the future of the human species. The reason this has become a threat to life on earth is that these are not acts of worship. These are not time spent in giving glory to God.

In essence, therefore, what an anointed leader is called to do is lead man back to the world *as time began*. The leader is to have the ability to lead the nation, company, military, church or school aware that time is a gift straight from the hand of God at creation. He is to make those he leads connect, in spirit, to the divine vision of a world at worship, a realm where in the marketplace and the State House, each decision is made only after dialing the boardrooms of heaven and hearing what the wise counsel is. It is because we are all connected to the beginning.

Seasons

Anointed leadership exposes a servant of the Lord to the ability to understand seasons. The leader has to be aware of the nature of times we live in and lead the flock to safety should there be danger lurking in the horizon. I recall the afternoon I walked up to my mentor in Uganda and told him I had come to the point I needed to go in a different direction in ministry. By this time, I had been a pastor for a couple of years and served as a missionary in in the pearl of Africa. There was a prodding, though, that had persisted in my heart and I could no longer put it off.

I wanted to go back to Kenya. So I went and discussed the matter with leaders of the church in Uganda.

I had read the season I was in and knew that the Lord was calling me to operate at a different level, to care for His flock from the elevation of a different season. He had provided the grace, the favor and everything else I needed to transition into that new season. There was no reason to linger in Uganda when the Lord was calling me to serve in Kenya. I had to listen to the counsel of Solomon who, after watching the world around him, warned the Israelites about seasons (Ecclesiastes 3:1-8, NIV).

There is a time for everything,
and a season for every activity under the heavens:

2 a time to be born and a time to die,
a time to plant and a time to uproot,
3 a time to kill and a time to heal,
a time to tear down and a time to build,
4 a time to weep and a time to laugh,
a time to mourn and a time to dance,
5 a time to scatter stones and a time to gather them,
a time to embrace and a time to refrain from embracing,
6 a time to search and a time to give up,
a time to keep and a time to throw away,
7 a time to tear and a time to mend,

> a time to be silent and a time to speak,
>
> 8   a time to love and a time to hate,
>
> a time for war and a time for peace.

Leadership is about having the temperament, judgement and wisdom to know when to change course. It is about correct timing. It is the rare quality of being guided by the Holy Spirit to send soldiers to the battlefield only after they have been provided with the weaponry to guarantee victory; the wisdom to pick Cabinet and Departmental officials whose only agenda is to implement policies that enrich the lives of God's children; the grace to remain connected to God as a church leader so that the flock are given the tools to become the salt of the earth.

The Apostle Paul, having understood the connectedness of time and the significance of seasons in a Christian's life, told the Corinthians to act within the grace of the season they were in. Listen to this:

> When I was a child, I spake as a child, I understood as a child, I thought as a child: but when I became a man, I put away childish things (1st Corinthians 13:11, KJV).

The apostle's admonition was that time demanded of a child the natural behavior of a child and of an adult the natural behavior of an adult. In like manner, a leader *needs* to behave as a leader and to understand the season his or her people are in. In poverty, people expect policies that eradicate poverty; during epidemics, people expect *quick* action to end the threat of spread; during war, people expect a robust offensive that ends aggression within the shortest time possible and with minimal civilian deaths or destruction of property. That is what understanding the times and seasons is all about.

Standing with the Giants

On the day we inaugurated the first Redeemed Gospel Church in Machakos, and lived in a humble house within the church compound, I looked back at the evening we buried my mother, the evening Dad was laid to rest and was gripped with a sense of urgency about the passage of time. As congratulatory messages were delivered, all I could think about was the many giants of faith who had occupied the very same space of time like I was, except that they had been here much earlier.

Time was the one *continuum* that had tied me, like an umbilical cord, to the anointed leaders of the past who acted to create an atmosphere of worship on earth. I was in the mold of Martin Luther, Abraham Lincoln, Nelson Mandela, Mahatma Gandhi and Pope John Paul II. These were the men and women who accepted the *gift of time with grace* and understood the urgency of the moment. Any leader today, who offers the children of God a pathway to worship, stands with these giants of the past. He or she *stands* with the kings, the prime ministers, the presidents, archbishops, pontiffs and generals who have sensed that ours is one world, connected through time, to the beginning, called only to one core mission – worship of God!

Bowing to Time Today

In most leadership books, authors suggest ideas about how to keep time. They talk about having a To-do-List, about setting a clock five minutes ahead, finding time to rest, and ensuring business associates and clients understand the importance of *their* time. The advice such authors give is great, but only if played within the context of Genesis 1:1. Having, therefore, dug into the crux of this foundational matter, I find no need to prescribe ways to observe time. Each anointed leader will come wired with the genes that cause him or her to understand time as the greatest gift given to man.

As leaders, therefore, we are to conduct ourselves in ways that glorify God for placing us in the world at this time. We are to treat each minute of life with the knowledge that it will never return, that as it slips by, it joins the rest of the minutes that have entered the realm of history and linked our present to acts of the past and acts of the future. What we do with our time this very second, therefore, has its place in the way it will impact destiny – and for that, God will hold us to account. This is why time was sanctified … so that in importance, it would rank right up there with human life.

Tick tock tick tock … !

SIX
PATIENCE

I recall the day I was sent to pastor a church in Fort Portal like it happened just yesterday. I had been in the ministry for a couple of months now and all indications were that I would remain an assistant in the Kampala area. The fear I once had about becoming a preacher had disappeared and I was looking forward to another great year of service. It finally felt like the Lord was dropping the sweet fruits of His reward from the tree of grace to me because I had unreservedly answered His call.

Suddenly, it got more specific.

I was asked to go to Fort Portal.

To a church in the Rwenzori area.

I didn't have a problem going to the western region of Uganda because I now saw myself as a servant of the Lord, a vessel ready to be used to grow the kingdom in any corner of the nation – and indeed in any corner of the world. Besides, I had come to the *realization* that when the

Lord called, the only question a shepherd needed to ask was – are there people there? If the answer was yes, I was to respond like Christians of old, who faced great odds and threats to life but came out to do the will of God nonetheless. I was to act like the Apostle Paul, he who abandoned his persecution of Christians and became one of the greatest Christian leaders of all time. I was to act like the Apostle Peter, he who became so zealous for the cause of Christ that upon him Christ founded the Church.

When I got to the new place, I ran into a dire situation. There was no church structure and no congregation to talk about. Seeing how dire the situation was, I had to set my mind on ideas and approaches that would inspire the people of the area to give themselves to Christ.

Within a couple of months, membership of the church rose significantly, but it wasn't without pain.

Today, as I look back at that moment – and many other moments in my life – I realize why the Lord brought me through the tunnel of childhood suffering, glory of life as a businessman and humility of surrendering my life to Him. God was preparing me for the days of leadership. He was shaping my future in the ministry, aware great patience was going to be required of me as a leader of His wounded flock in the age of speed and vast knowledge.

Nature of the Flock

The Lord knows the nature of the flock He calls us to lead. He is aware that we live in a broken world that has subjected us to *intense suffering, deep pain* and *endless tears*. He knows that death, sickness, poverty, and other calamities have sunk our spirits to depths unimaginable. This is what He said when He saw people one day:

> When he saw the crowds, he had compassion on them, because they were harassed and helpless, like sheep without a shepherd (Matthew 9:36, NIV).

All across Africa, Christ continues to look at His flock with *compassion* because He understands the suffering His people have been through.

a. **In the East African nation of Uganda,** a celebrated military coup brought to power a leader who later killed many Christians, businessmen and anybody who opposed his rule. He ruined the economy of the nation by dishonoring policies meant to grow the fragile economy of the nation. By the time he was deposed, he left behind a bleeding, wounded flock, a nation trapped in gloom.

b. **In South Africa,** the system of governance known as apartheid led to untold suffering as whites in the nation enacted rules that established segregation as the official practice in the land. To enforce these draconian rules, which were violently opposed by South African blacks and coloreds, Africans were met with *forceful* repression, murder, and sometimes torture. In, perhaps, the richest nation on the poor continent – with gold, copper and other minerals, and a temperate climate that supported citrus fruits and other crops of export value – Africans lived in abject poverty and squalor, trapped in the *sprawling* slum dwellings of Soweto and Johannesburg.

c. **In Angola,** the ruinous civil war that pitted Jonas Savimbi's guerilla forces against those of Edwardo Dos Santo's government caused endless spillage of blood as Angolans were subjected to the misery of failed crops, destruction of property, tribal *animosity* and underdeveloped infrastructure. The guns and bombs used in the war caused untold mayhem – and later the landmines left behind by armies intent on a scorched-earth policy killed and maimed many innocent civilians – some as they tilled the land.

d. **In Rwanda,** the *unforeseen* assassination of President Habyarimana unleashed a spate of killings that led to one of the most ferocious civil wars ever to be witnessed in Africa. As the Hutus turned on their Tutsi brothers, Rwanda was gripped by *bloodletting* on a scale no one imagined possible. When the guns went silent, more than one million people had been killed as the world watched.

In the West African region, nations like Liberia and Sierra Leon have borne the brunt of ruthless leadership. In the Central African region, the Central African Republic or CAR has known no moment of peace in the last couple of years; and in the Great Lakes Region, the Democratic Republic of Congo and Zaire have gone from one *pogrom* to another as insensitive regimes rule the land.

By the examples I have presented above, if you were to ask me the *nature* or *characteristics* of God's flock in Africa, I wouldn't hesitate in describing the flock as broken, weak and weary. God's people have faced *atrocities* and endured upheavals as demonic forces have used military generals and agented leaders to draw blood on the continent. In Rwanda, the bloodshed witnessed there was seen as the largest harvest of blood in modern times by the forces of evil. The valleys and basins of the land filled with the blood of God's people as their cracking voices were drowned out by the merciless sound of gunfire, explosives and commands. The nation was reeling!

Aware Africans have had to endure such pain, Christ has adopted the approach of patience in the way He ministers to Africa's mounting needs. He has ensured that the new men and women He calls to lead His wounded flock are anointed and tested for the enormous work ahead. He promises that as His people worship Him in the new dispensation He will have caused to be, healing and renewal will take place.

> Your people will rebuild the ancient ruins and will raise up the age-old foundations; you will be called Repairer of Broken Walls, Restorer of Streets with Dwellings (Isaiah 58:12).

It is only fitting that Christ should give this great promise of restoration to His people after the merciless suffering experienced in Africa over the years. For restoration to take place, He has moved the continent on a path to governance structures that will enable spirit-filled rule to take root. Patience is the virtue Heaven places the largest premium on as it moves to partner with those who will dry the tears of Africa as its anointed leaders.

It is, perhaps, in recognition of the broken nature of the flock that Christ presented His approach as one of gently pleading with the flock when He visited with John the Revelator in a vision. There, in the island of Patmos, He told the jailed leader of weary Christians that the spirit says come...

> And the Spirit and the bride say, Come. And let him that heareth say, Come. And let him that is athirst come. And whosoever will, let him take the water of life freely (Revelation 17:22, KJV).

He is calling the patient to leadership; not the cruel, the haughty or the highhanded. He has in His hand the water of life and He is presenting it freely to the flock. In this new realm, He will not call anyone to leadership that is not anointed to bear the great burden of patience in healing His wounded people.

The Meaning of Patience

It was after a well-attended service in Fort Portal. I had just delivered one of my sermons and people were leaving to go back to their homes. In that moment, I looked at the weary of the land and realized that what the Lord had called me to wasn't glamor but service. He had called me to heal wounds that had been caused by men and women who did not understand the nature of flock in their hands.

We are discussing patience.

What is it and what does it take?

On a matter of such pivotal importance, it is wise to excavate the meaning of *patience* by digging through the buried ruins of the deep past. What are its characteristic ingredients and do they exist in our world today – as it is presently constituted?

a. An intimate walk with God. An intimate walk with God is about living inside the mind of God, feeling what He feels and seeing the world through the prism of His lenses rather than man's. For this to happen, we have to remain in the mode of:

- Prayer, so that a relationship of friendship and deep trust is established. Prayer is the key to heaven, the power that connects man to the storehouse of abundance in grace, favor and other blessings of God. Prayer is the tool of thanksgiving, seeking blessings and conversing with God.

- Meekness, so that our minds and spirits are kept in the divine mode of *connectivity* with the hosts of heaven. Matthew picked up on the importance of this matter when he said: *Blessed are the meek, for they will inherit the earth* (Matthew 5:5, NIV). Leadership is about inheriting the earth on a caretaker basis, on a *stewardship* basis, until the Lord comes back to take care of His own.

- Wisdom, so that like King Solomon we be cast in the role of making all the right judgements, making all the *spirit-led* moves and having the inner eye of vision to see events before they occur. Others call this proactive leadership; I call it wisdom.

b. **Divine genetic disposition.** There is a certain level at which this is similar to having a closer walk with God, but a deeper examination reveals that divine genetic disposition is about creation, about the manner God fitted one to view the world and react to its many challenges. Biologists have helped the world understand the intricacy of genetics in the making of man and attributed it to inheritance of genetic characteristics from a biological father or mother. In the case of *anointed* leadership, however, God fits His servants with additional characteristics that will become helpful in navigating the hills and valleys of life created as traps by Satan. That new genetic mapping is what creates the disposition within an anointed leader to be in natural tune with God and matters of leading for salvation.

c. **Awareness of stakes.** An anointed leader is called to deal in matters of *life and death*, to make decisions and act in ways that reveal the *profundity* of Christ's sacrificial death on the cross. An anointed *president* will thus lead through laws and policies that create an atmosphere conducive for worship; an anointed chairman of a public or private corporation will create laws and by-laws that uphold human dignity and point workers to the greater need of all – the need to *worship* and *prepare* for the coming kingdom; an anointed spiritual leader will speak without fear or favor about the topical issues of his or her time. He or she will help a nation interpret God's desires without worrying about the sensibilities of the powers that be because on matters of life and death, there can be no sugarcoating.

The Apostle Paul was aware of the power of patience when he spoke to the Galatians. From the look of things, it was a great sermon that needed to be preached because of ongoing spats in the body of Christ. As he listed the great virtues of a life lived in accordance with Christ's love, he ticked off patience.

> But the fruit of the Spirit is love, joy, peace, **forbearance**, kindness, goodness, faithfulness, [23] gentleness and self-control. Against such things there is no law
> (Galatians 5:22-23 NIV).

Patience, as we have established, therefore, is at the heart of a leader's prayer-list. It is the greatest of the *characteristics* a leader needs when called to serve a broken people like the *people of Africa*. It is, thus, not enough that a president be elected by the popular vote or storm his way to the State House through the barrel of a gun; it is not enough that a corporate leader be elected by a majority of the delegates or a church leader be installed on the basis of a popularity contest disguised as the inner workings of the Holy Spirit – if a man or a woman is not anointed, he or she will become a curse to the people. The nation will go into a season of bloodletting, hunger and calamities; the church will go into a season of syncretism, theological prostitution and lack of the Holy Spirit; the corporate world will go into a season of economic recession, which may lead to a meltdown and the collapse of a sector.

All over Africa – and around the world – demonic forces have had a field-day installing so called leaders in nations, in corporations and in the church. These have been agents of the underworld – people whose lack of patience has led Africa through the perilous *hallways* of bloodshed, hunger, poor governance and ongoing shame. The time has come that each time there is a transition in church, state or the corporate world, Africans must go on their knees to seek the Lord's hand in ushering in the reign of patience.

The Alternative to Patience
Chaos.

The ruthlessness of African despots like Mobutu, Amin Dada, Habre and Taylor remains the subject of *amazement* the world over. These men, lords of impatience, killed and maimed many citizens in a misguided quest to stem off any form of opposition. They saw themselves as small gods and demanded reverence reserved for God.

They wanted to be worshiped!

Like other so called leaders, those who have instituted impatience as a tool of leadership, the fruits of *lack of grace* have manifested themselves early.

a. **Arrogance.** Whether in *church*, *state* or in the *corporate world,* such a leader reveals his or her character by the way he or she:

- Talks. In his or her speeches, the sense is created of being above the law, being great and untouchable. He or she talks down to people and makes them feel *small*. He or she creates the sense of being a god and must be worshiped.

- Makes decisions. In arrogance, such a leader *cobbles* together an inner Cabinet, usually of close family members and friends, and uses it to make all critical decisions affecting a nation, church or corporation. *Professionalism* is thrown out the window as nepotism, sycophancy, tribalism and ineptness takes center-stage. It is the equivalent of telling the led that the leader doesn't' care what they think. It inevitably leads to chaos.

- Amasses wealth. Without shame, such a leader amasses wealth by stealing from the nation or church or company and stashing the loot in foreign banks. This blind arrogance leads him or her to *parade* his or her family during national, church or corporate festivities to subjects languishing in poverty, ill-heath and desperation.

b. **Pride.** Pride is what causes a so called leader to imagine that he or she can be worshiped. It is what causes him or her to feel no need to consult widely on critical matters affecting a nation or church or corporation – and feels no need to seek God's help through prayer. Such a leader suffers the delusions experienced by tactless men like Nebuchadnezzar, Domitian, Caligula, Nero, Amin and Castro. They do well to remember the adage – pride goes before a fall. For Taylor, that fall led to imprisonment; for Amin, it led to exile; for Domitian, Caligula and Nero, it led to the end of empires. *Wisdom* is found in understanding that *leadership* is for the anointed; anyone who imposes on others will only become a curse to the nation, the church or the company.

c. **Hate.** Inevitably, deep hate will manifest in a so called leader because he or she will detest the voices of opposition that builds to repressive and unresponsive leadership. A hateful leader will move to contain any opposition by hatefully purging members of:

- A tribe perceived to be at the forefront of agitation for inclusive leadership. He or she will ensure that people from the offending tribe are reduced to a voiceless minority. In extreme cases, such a leader will instigate a state of strife in his church, company or in a nation to retain power.

- A religious group perceived to be *sympathetic* to voices of *opposition*. In Northern Ireland, the Catholics and Anglicans have been at it for years, leading to religious tensions that affect leadership. In Nigeria, the Islamic north and the Christian South have been at loggerheads since the beginning of modern Nigeria, leading to divisions. And around the world, ongoing efforts by radical Islam to establish a global caliphate have risen temperatures around the world to new highs in relation to religious intolerance. This has affected the manner leaders relate to subjects of different religious backgrounds. It manifests in hate.

- Social class perceived to be in the lead in calling for change. Inevitably, those who will champion inclusive leadership will be the left-behinds, those who feel left out in the nation's economic growth; in a church's expansion and leadership; in a company's sharing of profits and leadership positions; and in a military's nature of command structure. God created man to seek freedom so that in freedom he would worship the Creator in peace. Any system that oppresses man will inevitably be challenged. It may come down peacefully or it may come down tumbling in a chaotic manner – the choice is usually in the hands of the *despotic*, *dictatorial* and *hateful* leader.

The words of the Apostle Paul come to mind as we close this critical chapter. Aware that lack of patience affects the world in mighty ways, he ticked off *characteristics manifested* in those who lacked the virtue in Galatians 5:19-12 (NIV). This is scary:

> The acts of the flesh are obvious: sexual immorality, impurity and debauchery; [20] idolatry and witchcraft; *hatred*, discord, jealousy, *fits of rage,* selfish ambition, dissensions, factions [21] and *envy;* drunkenness, orgies, and the like. I warn you, as I did before, that

those who live like this will not inherit the kingdom of God (Italicized emphasis mine).

Africa's *hour of prayer* has come. We are to pray for leaders in our nations, our churches and our corporations who the Lord has anointed to bless His people. We are to end the reign of satanic leaders by prayerfully erecting a barrier of God's favor upon us by *electing* men and women we have examined their character; by *choosing* spiritual leaders we have observed the nature of their walk with God; and by *elevating* to corporate leadership only those who have been called to create wealth for the glory of the Lord.

The Lord is willing and stands ready to partner with Africa in ridding the continent of those who lack patience, those whose first answer to any challenge is threats. We are to welcome the new era of God's reign on the continent by *positioning ourselves* to be used by Him in this moment of laying a divine foundation for a buffer zone where *end-time* worship will take place on earth – right here in Africa.

SEVEN
INSPIRATION

In modern times, there has never been a leader more revered and respected the world over like the late Nelson Mandela. I was among the millions of people across the globe who stayed glued to my TV screen to watch each moment of events unfolding in South Africa as Africa's greatest son of the twentieth century was laid to rest. In life, as in death, Mandela galvanized the world to witness the substance of human greatness, the glory of bravery in humility and the endless possibilities in *goodness* that man could inspire if we lived true to God's vision of human dignity, love for all and uncompromising integrity.

As the sun set that evening in Africa, casting an orange beam across the land, there was a sense that the continent had lost immeasurably, that our children would grow up minus the benefit of having the towering figure as an adopted grandpa – a man who would shape their belief in themselves and teach them that in *humility*, there is *strength* and that integrity is all there is to a man or woman.

Many years after Nelson Mandela was born, a son of mixed heritage was born in the state of Hawaii, in the United States of America. The father was a Kenyan; the mother a white lady from Kansas. The world didn't know much about the boy until he became the United States Senator from the state of Illinois. Not one to forget his roots, he traveled to his father's native land of Kenya and was welcomed with gladness. He not only became an instant sensation, but he became an inspiration to people around the world about what focus and belief in oneself could achieve. As Mandela was entering his sunset years, Barack Obama was entering his prime years.

In 1994, the world stood still as the young, lanky Illinois senator took to the rapturous floor at the Democratic National Convention in Boston, Massachusetts, and gave a rousing speech that was to define the path he would later take to the Presidency of the most powerful nation on earth. He combined the incredible oratorical skills of Martin Luther King with the ringing message of a *hopeful*, united America and gave the nation a reason to believe that man could live in peace and dig deep to embrace at the table of brotherhood. He rekindled hope by inspiring Americans to remember what made that nation a beacon of hope around the world.

Four years later, David Axelrod and a couple of brilliant strategists molded Barack into a formidable candidate for

President of the United States. He went on to win the election and gave America her first black president. Throughout his two terms, Barack has been aware of the power of his office and has used it to inspire millions of people around the world. From his humble beginnings, he scaled the heights and believed not only in the greatness of the United States, but in the power of his dream. He inspired the world to believe that hard work, patience and integrity were the virtues it took to rise to greatness – and that the world was looking for men in that mold.

Inspiration Defined

In most leadership books, you will encounter definitions of this word as drawn from dictionaries and thesauruses. I have no quarrel with that. I, however, shudder at the sense that these definitions wholly miss the point. They fail to capture the deeper spirit of the word by connecting it to the roots of leadership – its roots in divinity. As a minister of the gospel, I have been compelled to study the meaning of this word for the sake of my church members. Indeed, when I first started this study, I thought I was doing it as an exercise in improving my leadership skills. I was wrong. It didn't take long to discover that I was dealing with a matter that is the only fulcrum upon which every virtue rotates in leadership. It is the center bolt!

One friend, when I asked him what the word meant, told me it is the ability to be so charismatic that when you tell someone to *go to hell*, he'd walk away gladly as he looked forward to the trip. A cynical view it is, but it makes the point. Another friend said inspiration was such a pivotal word in leadership that not too many leaders around the world have achieved it. As he talked about its *core elements*, I realized why he felt leaders had failed at it. In defining the world, I feel compelled to *highlight* those core elements so that we may establish an unshakable foundation for this critical discussion. Here are the *core elements* in inspiration:

a. **Ultimate source.** In an earlier chapter, we *determined* that there is only one LEADER and that all power and authority to lead is derived from Him. By virtue of being the creator and owner of all there is, God has extended an invitation to servants He has anointed to lead His people. Equally, we have also established that Satan has positioned himself as an alternative source of power (inspiration) and has led some people away from the vision of God. In Africa, and around the world, we know this:

- That any president, king or political leader who draws his or her power to inspire from God will lead like a shepherd. The people he or she leads will experience favor and grow in grace because their leadership is connected to the throne of glory. A king or president or any political leader who draws inspiration from Satan will cause bloodshed, cause destruction and cause tears.

- That any *church leader* who draws the power to inspire from the Lord will lead his or her people to greener pastures, where they will fatten in health and grow in strength. The flock will follow him or her because of his or her trustworthiness and ability to always steer them in the direction of safety. Church leaders who draw inspiration from Satan will only inspire death, destruction and pain in the flock. Children and women will cry in their name because they will ruin many lives and bury hope.

- That any corporate leader who draws the power to inspire from God will lead his or her team to create wealth and experience *tremendous* growth in profits because eager workers will see in the leader a connection to something divine – *manifested* in love for humanity. A corporate leader who draws inspiration from Satan may experience gains in the early days by engaging in satanic rituals or sacrifices, but the end is always assured because Satan comes to steal, kill and destroy.

b. **Understanding the stakes.** Because of sin, we live in a broken world, where the stakes could have never been higher for man. Satan and his agents have upped their game and are seeking destruction, killing; and are swaying many souls from God. It ultimately comes down to two matters:

- Vindication of God's *character of love,* which the demonic world has tried to cast as a lie. In the end, God will move in to restore His glory by destroying Satan and His vicious lies – but only after man will have been a witness to the *cynical* lies and *deadly* results of Satan's activities since he was sent packing.

- Eternity. As Christ left for heaven, perched on a cloud of glory, He said this: *My Father's house has many rooms; if that were not so, would I have told you that I am going there to prepare a place for you? ³And if I go and prepare a place for you, I will come back and take you to be with me that you also may be where I am. ⁴You know the way to the place where I am going* (John 14:2-4, NIV). The Lord, in love, has extended an invitation to us to share eternity with Him. Satan is *hell-bent* on denying us that opportunity and is enticing us with false *glory* and *wealth* so that we may one day perish with him as God cleanses the world of all sin.

c. **Vision.** Vision is the roadmap to the destination a leader is guiding his or her people to. It is the power to see what is coming and preparing people to know how to cope with it while keeping an eye on the ball. A great leader will inspire people to live within the hope and dream of achieving glory by following in the footsteps of Christ. He or she will demonstrate, by showcasing past greats who have achieved similar results, that *love, justice* and *fairness* are indeed within reach here on earth if we remain connected to the God of the beginning.

d. **Selflessness.** This is the ability to put the interests of others first; the desire to work tirelessly for the happiness and comfort of others. For twenty seven years, Nelson Mandela languished in prison so that his people could one day go free. In his ministry, Martin Luther King preached against racism in America at the risk of his own life. He was, indeed, felled by an assassin's cold bullet in Memphis on account of his vociferous opposition to inhumane laws in the books across the United States. To be selfless, one has to be filled with:

- Love, because this is the *sunshine* that makes us blind to color, tribe, religion, and social class as we look at its eye.

- Pity, because this is the *detergent* that washes away our sense of detachment and causes us to walk in the shoes of others.
- Drive, because this is the *accelerator* we must step hard on to free brothers and sisters afflicted by the pain of hunger, war, illness and hopelessness.
- Grace, because this is the *inner eye* that makes us see the world around us through the eyes of Christ and drives us to act in ways that lead people to salvation rather than lead them to doubt God's love.

Inspiration, as is evidenced by this long definition, is the ability to cheer the brokenhearted, uplift the comfortable and cause all groups of people to act as one in pursuit of salvation. I don't need to tell you that no human being, of one's accord, can inspire – this is a matter over which heaven must have a hand. The men and women who will inspire will have to have been anointed, called by God to carry the shepherd's rod as the sheep follow.

One of my strongest *inspirations* – through the years – has been my wife. I recall that before Gertrude and I got married, I cast my net in seas in Kenya for a suitable lady. I met a number of great ladies, but I failed to see one who was as promising as the lady I had met in Uganda. Aware of the stakes in serving God, I knew what I needed was a strong lady who loved God and was ready to live the highly demanding life of a pastor's wife. I asked the Lord to make it possible for Gertrude and I to get married and the Lord answered graciously.

Through the years, Gertrude has been a pillar in my life. She has prayed for me, fasted for the ministry, brought up our children and rebuked me when she felt I needed the loving rebuke of a wife. Together, we managed to balance family time and work time, sparing moments of reflection on child upbringing and other issues of importance to each other. She has been the captain that has steadied the ship of my life. Her strong partnership with God has been the inspiration that has brought me this far!

Urgency to Inspire

In Africa, as in other places, there are three areas people have needed to be inspired in. These are the pillars that enable a society to function and are the reason a society will rise or fall – depending on how they are treated. Of the three giant pillars, the one that needs the most urgent inspiration is the church.

   a. **The church.** Christ established the church so that it would stand in for Him as the voice of hope and reason in a world of *pain*, *disagreements* and enduring *hopelessness*. In most regions of Africa, and around the world, the church has, however, become an enabler of evil tendencies, encouraged nepotistic policies and fallen deep into syncretism. The voice of hope it could have offered has been muzzled by the actions of church leaders whose morals are of questionable *quality*, whose prayers are of a shallow *nature*, and whose patterns in life mirror those of the world rather than those of heaven. Among the key issues the church must battle are:

- Immorality. Just as the days of the Apostle Paul, sexual and other forms of immorality have continued in the church. Pastors, lay people and elders have engaged in sexual relations and weakened the church's voice. Like back then, this matter remains *so serious* that the words of admonition the apostle sounded remain relevant. *Or do you not know that the unrighteous will not inherit the kingdom of God? Do not be deceived: neither the sexually immoral, nor idolaters, nor adulterers, nor men who practice homosexuality, nor thieves, nor the greedy, nor drunkards, nor revilers, nor swindlers will inherit the kingdom of God (1ˢᵗ Corinthians 6:9-10, NIV).*

- Misappropriation of funds. This is the *act* of using tithe and offerings for personal gain rather than for their intended *purposes*. Many pastors and elders have used church monies to buy sleek cars, purchase expensive homes and support a lifestyle wholly inappropriate of a servant of God. In the story of Ananias and Sapphira, the Lord is issuing a warning. The story is in Acts 5:1-11 (NIV).

Now a man named Ananias, together with his wife Sapphira, also sold a piece of property. ² With his wife's full knowledge he kept back part of the money for himself, but brought the rest and put it at the apostles' feet.

³ Then Peter said, "Ananias, how is it that Satan has so filled your heart that you have lied to the Holy Spirit and have kept for yourself some of the money you received for the land? ⁴ Didn't it belong to you before it was sold? And after it was sold, wasn't the money at your disposal? What made you think of doing such a thing? You have not lied just to human beings but to God."

⁵ When Ananias heard this, he fell down and died. And great fear seized all who heard what had happened. ⁶ Then some young men came forward, wrapped up his body, and carried him out and buried him.

⁷ About three hours later his wife came in, not knowing what had happened.⁸ Peter asked her, "Tell me, is this the price you and Ananias got for the land?"

"Yes," she said, "that is the price."

⁹ Peter said to her, "How could you conspire to test the Spirit of the Lord? Listen! The feet of the men who buried your husband are at the door, and they will carry you out also."

¹⁰ At that moment she fell down at his feet and died. Then the young men came in and, finding her dead, carried her out and buried her beside her husband. ¹¹ Great fear seized the whole church and all who heard about these events.

I need not add a word to this!

- Fighting for leadership. The open season of *fights for leadership* in the church has gravely *undermined* the church's ability to stand apart as an entity that operates on the principles of heaven. There is no difference between pastors who clamor for leadership and the cold acts of Lucifer, who caused rebellion in heaven by seeking to be like God. If the Lord be the Lord of the church, He must be the one to pick leaders He has anointed and wired to lead His people. Those who campaign, canvas and lobby for leadership may eventually get to leadership, as Satan creates a pathway for them, but they will never lead God's people to true worship.

b. **The state.** This is a territory curved out by borders and is defined under *international* systems as a *nation*. In Africa, there are more than fifty of such units, each with a president and those who serve under him or her. Africa's endemic problems are caused and exacerbated by this class of people. They lack inspiration in the core areas of:

- Service delivery. As monies generated from the internal economy, the World Bank and the International Monetary Fund are stolen, the services Africans expect *are never delivered*. Healthcare, national security, food security, a *robust* infrastructure and economic growth are stunted amid poor governance.

- International cooperation. One of the key tasks of a government is to establish cordial relations with *nations* and *institutions* around the world. Bilateral ties with critical nations must be enhanced as multilateral ties are sought with potential nations that Africa stands to gain from. Because of timidity on the world stage, however, Africa's foreign ministers and presidents fail to meaningfully interact with democratic nations and key global institutions that our nations could benefit from. It is lack of *inspired leadership*.

- Innovation. Innovation is the act of using resources one has in hand to make critical *advances*. Africa has been called the sleeping giant because of her failure to innovatively interact with its vast resources in copper, gold, aluminum, iron, vast agricultural land and *human capital* to create *wealth*. Prosperity has eluded us on account of poor *governance*, endless reliance on foreign ideas and the silent mentality that whites are better than us. The leader Africa's young nations need is one who will realize and harness the full potential of available resources so that life may improve as services are delivered in a timely and professional manner.

- Negative ethnicity. In almost all the nations in Africa, negative ethnicity or tribalism has been a cancer that has continued to eat the fabric of national unity. It has encouraged negative trends like nepotism, favoritism, separation and other vices of our time. This is a cancer Africa's new leaders have to deal with so that nations united for the common good of the continent may emerge.

c. **Corporate Africa.** Like the state, corporate Africa is mired in negative ethnicity, in lack of innovation, and in failure to be imaginative. State firms and private firms have failed to perform because those entrusted with the responsibility to lead have neither been *competitively selected* nor held to account for endemic poor performance.

It is in consideration of the hole Africa is in – with regard to these three pillars – that we talk about urgency to prayerfully seek leaders who will inspire citizens. Leaders in the church, the state and corporations have to remain *connected* to God as the only source of inspiration so that through them, God may pour His favor on the people.

The model of Christ

Come to Me, all who are weary and heavy-laden, and I will give you rest. "Take My yoke upon you and learn from Me, for I am gentle and humble in heart, and YOU WILL FIND REST FOR YOUR SOULS. "For

My yoke is easy and My burden is light (Matthew 11:28-30, NIV).

In all His undertakings on earth, Christ was guided by the force of compassion. It made Him connect with the needs and fears of those He served. As He rolled up His sleeves and got into the trenches to ease their burden, He inspired them by His deep care for them. More than any other *style of leadership*, this model of compassion is the most fitting for Africa. It is responsive to the needs of the people and empathizes with their plight. It is the kind of leadership that inspires because it does four critical things:

    a. Cares. And Jesus called His disciples to Him, and said, "I feel compassion for the people, because they have remained with Me now three days and have nothing to eat; and I do not want to send them away hungry, for they might faint on the way (Matthew 15:32, NIV).

    b. Empathizes. In all their affliction He was afflicted, And the angel of His presence saved them; In His love and in His mercy He redeemed them, And He lifted them and carried them all the days of old (Isaiah 63:9, NIV).

    c. Touches. Jesus stretched out His hand and *touched* him, saying, "I am willing; be cleansed." And immediately his leprosy was cleansed (Matthew 8:3, NIV).

d. **Lives the experience of others.** Therefore, He had to be made like His brethren in all things, so that He might become a merciful and faithful high priest in things pertaining to God, to make propitiation for the sins of the people (Hebrews 2:17, NIV).

Compassion is a deep and critical element of inspiration. It is the substance that interacts with the emotion, intellect and perception of the led to cause them to believe that a leader indeed cares for them. When those who are led are satisfied that their leader is a compassionate, caring man or woman, they stand ready to offer their most-prized passion – trust. It is this trust that awakens the deeper realm known as inspiration as those who are led finally follow the guidance of a trusted, faithful leader. It is called servant-leadership – one that goes deep down the trenches to improve the lives of the led.

Christ used this model and presented the powerful image of a shepherd that was followed by the sheep. Here in Africa, we are used to a situation where the sheep or cows are driven to the grazing fields or water sources by the shepherd, but among the Jews it was the exact opposite, where the kind shepherd walked ahead of the sheep and led them to the best pastures of the field, where they ate to their fill. This model was what Christ demonstrated when He gave us the Jewish shepherd as the leader to emulate in taking care of God's people.

For those who are the weakest, He goes an extra mile: *Like a shepherd He will tend His flock, In His arm He will gather the lambs And carry them in His bosom; He will gently lead the nursing ewes* (40:11, NIV). This powerful model of leadership is what a land in dire need of healing craves. From the state house to the church headquarters; and from a chancellor's office to a corporation's head office, the Lord is inviting men and women filled with compassion and wired to feel the pain of His children to rise up and take leadership. He is seeking a new breed of leaders, those who will inspire His children to believe in the power of grace.

Inspiration Today

On the day I huddled with Arthur Kitonga, the dynamic preacher whose interest was to set up base in Nairobi's Mathare Valley, we agreed that we needed to serve the Lord on a different level. I had come back from Uganda empowered by the Holy Spirit to carry the message of the cross to my motherland, but I needed someone to partner with. I found that someone in Arthur.

In a matter of months, we registered Redeemed Gospel Church and agreed to divide the missionary field into the Nairobi area, which Arthur was going to minister to, and the Machakos area, which I was going to handle. On that basis, the Lord moved in to establish our credentials as leaders called to inspire His children.

The Lord asked Arthur and I to establish a body of Christ that would focus heavily on training leaders for His flock. It would then cast them in the broader field to grow the kingdom. We deliberately patterned our operations after the Ugandan model and sensed at once that it would require all the grace heaven could pour on us. We weren't scared, however, because the call came with *sufficient grace*.

It came with an abundance of favor!

As our vision slowly caught on, catalyzed by the spirit-led excitement in our fresh approach to ministry, the church we founded grew in leaps and bounds. Our forays into high schools and colleges yielded a harvest of souls as young people dedicated themselves to service.

Relying on inspiration from On High, we galvanized the newly-faithful and revealed the vast new realm the Lord was opening up. Within a short time, we built an amazing movement in the heart of Kenya and set out to make the movement spread out into all the regions of the nation – and later to all corners of Africa. We were going to inspire a new generation of African leaders and church faithful to do God's work wherever they were. The Lord was coming soon and we needed to prepare a people!

Today, as I look back at that humble beginning, I realize that the greatest burden Africa has had to bear is that of being trapped under the leadership of men and women without the slightest ability to inspire anyone. With their *thoughtlessness* guiding their actions, leaders have perfected the art of killing, destroying and stealing – making it all but impossible for inspiration to flow from them to the people they lead. They have failed to earn the trust of the people, thus finding need to rely on unorthodox means to coerce following. Their philosophy of leadership is built on the draconian idea that respect is forced, not earned. The truth is – any leader who fails to lead like a trusted Jewish shepherd, from the front, has failed to prepare his or her people for worship.

———

Inability to inspire inevitably releases the most negative consequences on those burdened by leadership imposed through manipulated processes. On a national level, it may set the stage for assassinations, detentions, sectarian strife, tribalism, nepotism and other vices. In the church, it may set the stage for doctrinal and territorial warfare, leading to splits in the body of Christ. In the corporate world, it may set the stage for nepotism, the plunder of resources and carelessness in matters of productivity. Such lack of inspiration inevitably leads to pain and suffering. It slows down worship!

It is, thus, important to warn those who cause tears to "the least of these" that God is in the business of keeping score. Listen to this:

> You have taken account of my wanderings; Put my tears in Your bottle Are they not in Your book? (Psalms 56:8, NIV).

And to this:

> ...for the Lamb in the center of the throne will be their shepherd, and will guide them to springs of the water of life; and God will wipe every tear from their eyes (Revelation 7:17, NIV).

And finally to this:

> ... and He will wipe away every tear from their eyes; and there will no longer be any death; there will no longer be any mourning, or crying, or pain; the first things have passed away (Revelation 21:4, NIV).

The concept of bottled tears originated among the Jews, who cried into bottles whenever a matter was so grave.

When men went to war, for example, their wives cried into a bottle and kept it till they returned. It was this concept that David brought to God as He pleaded that the Lord keep the tears caused by his enemies in a bottle. Failed leadership in the state, church and corporate Africa has caused tears the size of an ocean in this land. Woe unto the leaders who by failing to inspire have caused tears to be shed in God's land!

EIGHT
INNOVATION

One of the most powerful movies you will ever watch is *The Passion of the Christ*. Directed by Mel Gibson, the movie boasts the star-studded cast of actors Jim Caviezel as Jesus of Nazareth, Monica Bellucci as Mary Magdalene, Maia Morgenstern as Mary the mother of Jesus, and cold-eyed Hristo Shopov as Pontius Pilate. The life and times of the Son of God is narrated with breathtaking clarity to present the most vivid portrait of suffering and the need for fallen man to return to the Savior. In an effort to create desired effects in the motion picture, Director Gibson uses the most innovative technology of the time to recreate the Middle Eastern landscape as closely as possible.

Throughout the world, *innovation* has become the *watchword* in government circles, in the corporate world and in the church. Because of the impact of technological advances, it is fair to imagine that innovation came with computers, IPhones, IPads, MiPads and other gizmos of the modern age. Far from it. Innovation was set in motion the week

God created the heavens and the earth. In breathtaking detail, the writer of the book of Genesis describes the way the Creator spoke the firmament, the seas and the dry land into existence. He proceeded to fill these places with fishes of all types in the waters, animals large and small on dry land and birds of all colors in the skies. On the sixth day, He created Adam, then caused a deep sleep to come over him as the first surgical operation was performed to bring Eve into existence. It was innovation at its best.

On the seventh day, the Creator took a deserved break to assess what He had created. He loved what He saw and pronounced it good. Archeologists and other observers of biblical-times events have debated the possible location of the Garden of Eden and agreed that it may have been placed somewhere in the present-day Iraq, but consensus is yet to emerge on that being the definite location. What there is agreement on is the fact that the garden that left the hand of God was an all-time masterpiece, a garden whose rivers, flowers, skies and trees reflected the creative genius of a masterful innovator.

In Genesis 1:1-31 (NIV), the story of creation is recorded for us to get into the mind of the innovator, feel the *power* of a mind that could figure out the manner in which the waters of the garden, its beautiful leaves and fascinating aquatic life would operate in choreographed harmony. To set the stage for the discussion in this chapter, we need to read Genesis 1:1-31 – so we may be in the moment.

> In the beginning, God created the heavens and the earth. [2] The earth was without form and void, and darkness was over the face of the deep. And the Spirit of God was hovering over the face of the waters.
>
> [3] And God said, "Let there be light," and there was light. [4] And God saw that the light was good. And God separated the light from the darkness. [5] God called the light Day, and the darkness he called Night. And there was evening and there was morning, the first day.
>
> [6] And God said, "Let there be an expanse in the midst of the waters, and let it separate the waters from the waters." [7] And God made the expanse and separated the waters that were under the expanse from the waters that were above the expanse. And it was so. [8] And God called the expanse Heaven. And there was evening and there was morning, the second day.
>
> [9] And God said, "Let the waters under the heavens be gathered together into one place, and let the dry land appear." And it was so. [10] God called the dry land Earth, and the waters that were gathered together he called Seas. And God saw that it was good.
>
> [11] And God said, "Let the earth sprout vegetation, plants yielding seed, and fruit trees bearing fruit in

which is their seed, each according to its kind, on the earth." And it was so. [12] The earth brought forth vegetation, plants yielding seed according to their own kinds, and trees bearing fruit in which is their seed, each according to its kind. And God saw that it was good. [13] And there was evening and there was morning, the third day.

[14] And God said, "Let there be lights in the expanse of the heavens to separate the day from the night. And let them be for signs and for seasons, and for days and years, [15] and let them be lights in the expanse of the heavens to give light upon the earth." And it was so. [16] And God made the two great lights – the greater light to rule the day and the lesser light to rule the night – and the stars. [17] And God set them in the expanse of the heavens to give light on the earth, [18] to rule over the day and over the night, and to separate the light from the darkness. And God saw that it was good. [19] And there was evening and there was morning, the fourth day.

[20] And God said, "Let the waters swarm with swarms of living creatures, and let birds fly above the earth across the expanse of the heavens." [21] So God created the great sea creatures and every living creature that moves, with which the waters swarm, according to their kinds, and every winged bird according to its kind. And God saw that it was good. [22] And God blessed them, saying,

"Be fruitful and multiply and fill the waters in the seas, and let birds multiply on the earth." [23] And there was evening and there was morning, the fifth day.

[24] And God said, "Let the earth bring forth living creatures according to their kinds – livestock and creeping things and beasts of the earth according to their kinds." And it was so. [25] And God made the beasts of the earth according to their kinds and the livestock according to their kinds, and everything that creeps on the ground according to its kind. And God saw that it was good.

[26] Then God said, "Let us make man in our image, after our likeness. And let them have dominion over the fish of the sea and over the birds of the heavens and over the livestock and over all the earth and over every creeping thing that creeps on the earth."

[27] So God created man in his own image,
in the image of God he created him;
male and female he created them.

[28] And God blessed them. And God said to them, "Be fruitful and multiply and fill the earth and subdue it, and have dominion over the fish of the sea and over the birds of the heavens and over every living thing that moves on the earth." [29] And God said, "Behold, I have given you every plant yielding seed that is on the face of all the earth, and every tree with seed in its fruit. You shall have them for food. [30] And to every beast of the

earth and to every bird of the heavens and to everything that creeps on the earth, everything that has the breath of life, I have given every green plant for food." And it was so. [31] And God saw everything that he had made, and behold, it was very good. And there was evening and there was morning, the sixth day.

This is innovation at its best!

Many years later, Archbishop Arthur Kitonga and I have presided over a growing movement that has left behind earlier approaches we used as *technology* has been embraced by modern church workers. We have started hospitals, schools and instituted programs to care for the needy in society. All these endeavors have been driven on the wheels of greater technology and manifest innovativeness. The Church has evolved into a force that must run on the basis of best practices to compete in a brave, new world. So then … what is innovation?

Innovation Defined

Scholars in leadership will, no doubt, find it amazing that such a modern concept as innovation may be traced back to the very beginning of time. If, however, they took time to peel off the layers of the word, they will discover that indeed the first *manifestations* of innovation were observed when the world was created. This makes the concept have its roots – not in modern technology – but in divine creativity and God's grace to keep man discovering new ways of doing things to make life better. Innovation, thus, is a gift God gave each of us to bless us by engaging our minds in the pursuit of solutions to some of the most vexing problems of our time. As we did with inspiration, we are going to define innovation by its core characteristics – by its manifestations today.

    a. **Innovation takes thinking.** God has designed man in a way that thinking should come naturally. The human brain is the *most complex organ* ever created. It comes fitted with the ability to imagine and act in a way that continues the process of creation. The idea is that God knew – after the fall – that sin introduced a new element into the mix: decay. If things were left to themselves, there would be death, decay and ultimately chaos. By creating man with the capacity to think, He made certain that even in the state of sin, renewal would take place; that limited restoration would be assured. It was in recognition of the complex nature of the brain that David praised the Lord. *I will praise thee; for I am fearfully and wonderfully made: marvellous are thy works; and that my soul knoweth right well* (Psalms 139:14, KJV). To think, however, one needs certain basics.

- Conducive environment. I remain *convinced* that one of the reasons Africa has lagged behind in development and innovation is the deadly environment we find ourselves in. It is not an easy thing to think when bullets fly, bombs explode and epidemics threaten to wipe out a village. Any leader with an eye on innovation will enact laws and policies friendly to peace so that men and women can think things through.
- Support. Leadership is about providing an infrastructure that enables thinking to take place. Support in the form of availing great books, latest computers, equipped libraries and appropriate work stations is *something* a church, a company and a nation needs to invest in so that Africa too will start to boast great thinkers in the mold of Bill Gates and Sir Isaac Newton. It, of course, doesn't hurt anything to avail funds for research and studies aimed at improving the situation in Africa.

b. Innovation solves problems. The greatest problem that there has ever been is the sin problem. The fall of man ushered in an era of problems on all fronts.

- Illness. In Africa, illnesses of a nature never before known to man have caused death on an *epidemic* basis. Ebola, HIV-AIDS, cholera and other killers have invaded our space. Children have not been spared either. *Infant mortality* rates have dropped significantly, but before the latest medical breakthroughs, children died in Africa in droves, killed by measles, dehydration, child abuse and other treatable diseases.

- Social *upheavals*. Africa, as well as the world, has had to cope with *malevolence* among the youth, rebelliousness to laws and societal norms; and increased permissiveness in the nature of sexual relations. Everywhere one looks, systems are breaking down as people challenge rules and norms that have given societies a sense of direction.

- Political turmoil. This has been an ongoing problem in Africa. The continent has had its fair share of military coups, *assassinations*, ethnic cleansing, nepotism and meltdowns.

Civil wars have *decimated* whole populations as rival groups fight to control power and state resources. Ideological differences have been *catapulted* to the cynical level of enmity, causing tribal animosity and civil strife.

- Spiritual decline. Is it any wonder, therefore, that in the face of such upheavals humanity has lost faith in the existence of God? Is it any wonder that great theological concepts like *omnipotence, omnipresence* and *omniscience* have come to mean nothing more than big words? Can Africans be blamed for losing faith in a deity who seems disinterested in their problems? Because this is a matter that touches on salvation and eternity, it is an urgent problem that needs leadership of a nature only heaven can fashion out.

Innovation, thus, is the gift given to man to solve key problems sin has caused since the fall. As the demonic world *invents* new calamities and upheavals to torment man with – so that man's faith in God is steadily undermined – the grace of innovation is poured out in equal measure so that the children of God are taken care of.

c. **Innovation is a gift of the Spirit.** In His wisdom, the Lord has wired each of us to accomplish *specific* tasks on earth. There are those among us who have been called to be great innovators, to see the bigger picture, to find solutions to emerging problems. These are the men like the late Steve Jobs, who led Apple to lead in the realm of technological advancement by giving the world IPad, IMac and other gizmos. Innovative women like Carly Fiorina, the former CEO of Hewlett-Packard, have *immeasurably* moved the world forward by innovatively seeking answers to technologies that solve some of our modern-day problems. Just like others are called to be teachers, pastors, administrators and healers, so have these men and women in innovation been called to bless the children of God through carrying on with the process of creation. Their calling is to make the world a better place by giving us technologies and ideas designed to make life easier in an otherwise broken, wounded world.

d. **Innovation is endless.** The great partnership God has forged with man to keep the world *safe* through innovation will never end – not until the end of time. On that day, the Lord will move in to restore the world back to the glory it lost when the Garden of Eden was desecrated with sin. Until then, those called to find solutions to man's problems, through innovation, will remain busy. They will seek ways to cure new diseases, contain juvenile restlessness, end political upheavals and find ways to reconnect man with lost faith in the Creator. In this sense, it is easy to see that we are all called to be creative in the way we handle our assignments.

- The politician has to seek innovative ways of delivering services to *constituents*. Roads, hospitals, schools, churches and other *social* amenities are to be innovatively availed to the people as creativity is enlisted in the great effort to improve lives.
- The corporate leader has to seek innovative ways of increasing *productivity* and ensuring the quality of products is excellent. In a cold market, increasingly driven by critical performance measures such as profits, the external and internal environments; and the impact on society by a firm, innovation is the only way a company can remain on the cutting edge of technology and systems needed to achieve growth.

- The church leader has to seek innovative ways of introducing Christ to a generation of cynics. Religion has become suspect in a world that seeks answers to problems it appears unable to solve. To reach the cynic, the new church leader must embrace new and innovative ideas. He or she must use forums like social media, gadgets like IPads and even traditional media like radio, TV and newspapers. Through innovative ideas, the church leader must declare an all-out war on Satan and the corrupting influences his agents have suffocated the world with.

e. **Innovation may be abused**. The point needs to be made clear that the demonic world is in an active mode when it comes to innovation. Agents of the great deceiver (Satan) have infiltrated the world of technological advances and introduced elements designed to corrupt the mind of man. Children have been put at a great risk by companies that lace all games and programs with satanic stuff. The idea is to make sexual perversion, satanic rituals, bizarre orgies and blasphemy appear normal and even *cool*. The wise and the discerning will have the eyes and the ears to detect when innovation has ceased to be of God and has crossed the line to be a tool in the hands of demons. It calls for grace.

That has been a long definition, but it is one for which we had to indulge time. Innovation has become so critical in our world today that any leader with a desire to lead well has to embrace it. African leaders – in whatever sphere – have to welcome technological advancement and treat it as an ally in the ceaseless effort of service delivery and problem-solving. Nations, churches and companies that embrace innovation in leadership will walk proudly through the twenty-first century as problems are solved, advancements are made and people are happier.

Innovation and the End of Time

> But thou, O Daniel, shut up the words and seal the book, even to the time of the end. Many shall run to and fro, and knowledge shall be increased (Daniel 12:4, KJV).

By design, the Lord *anticipated* that in the time of the end, knowledge would increase and men would run to and fro. What Daniel was shown was twofold:

a. **That in the time of the end,** one of the signs that Christ's return was *drawing* nigh would be increased knowledge – evidenced by *unprecedented* innovation. In the history of mankind, I can't recall any time that man has been so far gone in technology and quality of life. Sample this:

- In the realm of warfare, we have invented nuclear arms, built supersonic jetfighters like the F-16s and B-52 bombers; increased capacity for intelligence-gathering and a 24-hour surveillance; and formed global pacts like NATO, ECOWAS and APEC to, *among other things*, minimize the prospects of war around the world.

- In the realm of medicine, we have made incredible discoveries in drugs, vaccines and causes of various illnesses that afflict man. We have invented great machines that make it easy to treat illnesses that could not be treated before. *Medical technology* has brought man to the place where certain forms of cancers and heart conditions can now be treated and life prolonged. *Diabetes Mellitus*, a known killer of the past, has now been contained as insulin and other drugs – along with other measures – are introduced to help patients live harmoniously with the challenging condition.

- In the realm of politics, we have introduced democracy as the best form of governance. The era of military coups and assassinations has been left behind as Africa *embraces* new approaches to leadership.

b. A warning. Daniel was shown that in the days of the end, increased knowledge was going to cause man to run to and fro in search of glory. He was supposed to sound a warning to the world that technological advancement and innovation were going to pose a danger to spiritual growth. It has indeed come to pass because today many are lovers of IPads and IMacs rather than lovers of God. We adore fancy engine-cars, breathtaking architecture, dizzying road networks and the fastest jet planes. Daniel's brief is to warn that in that very moment when we will be so taken with technology, Christ will move in to end it all as restoration takes place.

The Lord is not asking any of us to remain docile and view innovation with *suspicion*. He is not asking us to treat innovation as something evil. He is asking that as we interact with technology and embrace innovation, we remain alert to the corrupting influences it comes with. He is asking us to guard our minds against the secret satanic elements added to programs and software so that we are constantly bombarded by evil.

Leadership in the modern world requires those who will be able to *harness* the power of technology and innovation for the good of mankind. Diseases and political upheavals will be brought under control when anointed leaders act to channel the incredible power of innovation to causes of a worthy nature. Churches will flourish when pastors and elders use technology creatively to warn the world of the days of the end. Our mantra ought to be – if God gave man the brains to invent the NASA telescopes, the roaring fighter jets, the medical machines and IPads, it is because He wanted His children to be at the forefront of using technology and innovation to spread the good tidings of man's salvation. He wanted us to worship Him.

An anointed leader will instinctively respond to the itch within him or her to act on the still voice that demands embrace of technology and innovation to spread the love of God. He or she will see innovation as one of the final gifts the Creator has given man ahead of the rapture so that through innovation, many more souls will be drawn to Christ. That is the *substance* of 21st century of leadership.

NINE
COMMUNICATION

The stadium was packed with grieving South Africans and dignitaries from around the world – among them heads of state, diplomats and leaders of some of the world's largest companies. They were in South Africa to mourn the fallen giant, Nelson Mandela. The event was a celebration of life, but by the great sadness it generated, it was easily more of deep loss than celebration. The world watched in awe as dignitaries took turns praising the exploits of one of the twentieth century's most iconic figures, praising his toughness and resilience in the face of incredible odds.

In a moment like that, however, only a son of the soil had the capacity to get deep into the nature and scope of the loss South Africans were experiencing. When the Master of Ceremony, Secretary-General of the African National Congress, Cyril Ramaphosa, invited President Jacob Zuma to speak, the man neither got up nor acknowledged the gathered dignitaries. He was given the microphone, right where he sat, and waited till the stadium fell dead silent. A pin could be heard dropping.

President Obama was in the audience.

So was UN Secretary-General Ban Ki Moon.

Leaders from South American nations, not usually known to have any business in Africa, were also present.

Mandela had gathered the world.

President Zuma wasn't at it long. He invoked one of the shortest Zulu songs reserved for a fallen hero. In his deep voice, the President captured centuries of rich tradition, causing the nation to reflect on the magnitude of the loss. In that moment, not one dry eye could be seen in the stadium among South Africans. They felt the words, felt the deep loss, felt the president's pain.

The dirge spoke!

Through that incredibly powerful Zulu dirge, President Zuma communicated in a way he would never have had he chosen to get up to speak. What he demonstrated that day was mastery of the art of communication, an art each leader does well to cultivate. In a day and age when too many issues compete for man's attention, it is crucial to have a leader with the ability to speak above the noise and communicate in ways that have an impact.

Watching President Zuma that day, I could tell he had *sacked* all oxygen out of the room by the way he presented that timeless dirge – giving it deep credibility by his age, friendship with the fallen giant, and the painful feeling of being *orphaned*, which a broken nation felt. Like a wounded general, the dirge communicated the sense that in spite of the death of Mandela, the nation would go on under his leadership and that Zuma would walk in the shoes of the hero – a feat he appeared to lament about, because he felt the burden of fitting in the big shoes.

Communication Defined

Scholars in the field of communication have given us great definitions of the term. They have refined it so that it now appears to make sense to a modern student of words. In this evolving narrative, however, we have adopted the practice of defining terms by the characteristics they bear. Communication is one of the richest terms in leadership, one that has the ability to make or break. To define it in an effective manner, we have to *interrogate* the ingredients it comes with that make a communicator either great or mediocre or just plain out incapable.

In the fifty three years I have been in the ministry, I have come to learn that there is one core message we are all called to pass along. It is the message that the Lord has been, is today and will always be. His precepts and nature will never change. He is the same yesterday, today and tomorrow. Those who invent new theologies, *philosophies* and teachings regarding His fundamental principles are acting outside the framework of what He has revealed about Himself in Scripture, in Nature and Revelation.

The inspiring message of an eternal and unchanging God is the message we are to communicate to a broken world. As leaders is this cause, we are to train ourselves in ways that will effectively communicate that message. We are to equip ourselves with techniques relevant to handling those we are passing the message to.

a. **Reading the mood of an audience.** This is the most important rule of communication. A leader has to have the ability to read the mood of people so that the intended message is communicated. Whether one is the head of state, a spiritual leader or even a corporate head, understanding *mood* is essential and may mean everything in the long run. Some of the key moods to watch are:

- Sadness. President Zuma understood the gravity of the moment when Mandela died. He sensed the deep sadness in South Africa as people reflected on the passing of a man who had given one quarter of his life up to liberate them. In that poignant moment, he couldn't speak – he delved into a dirge. When people are sad, speak to the sadness.

- Happiness. In Hyde Park, Chicago, Illinois, the world watched in awe as President-elect Barack Obama led his family to the stage to thank Americans for electing him the forty third president of the most powerful nation on earth. It was a moment of jubilation for a society that had grappled with racism and was appearing to triumph over it. Humbled by what he saw, his soaring rhetoric faded as he looked ahead to the meaning of what had just happened. He spoke to history!

- Anger. In Paris, France, the stadium was *full* when terrorists struck. In a night of horror, they detonated explosives and killed more than one hundred people. In the aftermath, the nation got so angry that the President, Francois Hollande, took upon himself the role of a shuttle diplomat to rally the world to the urgent cause of defeating ISIS, which claimed responsibility for the attack. When he spoke to France, Hollande's words of defiance, somberness and fury galvanized a seething nation to be on a war footing.

- Contentment. The other word is *complacency*. It is what happens when life seems to be going well – with *minimum* threats, *maximum* benefits and a clear horizon. It is more of an issue in churches, where *syncretic tendencies* may creep in because of contentment. It may also become an issue in a company when profits are at an all-time high and worries are driven to the background. It can *afflict* a nation when leadership is responsive to the needs of citizens. In and of itself, contentment is not necessarily a bad thing, but when it distracts people from doing what is necessary, it becomes a danger. A wise leader has to know the right words to use when contentment has gripped people.
- Despair. This is the situation in much of Africa, where each elective season is a time of grave peril. The continent is led by men

who have no desire to step aside even after defeat – and some change laws to favor a third term where the Constitution allows two. It has happened in Burundi, Rwanda, Uganda … and we have not had the end of this negative trend. I don't know what a president whose nation he has caused to despair says to citizens, but I know that spiritual leaders in that nation are called to speak to the ills and address the despair of citizens even if it is at the risk of arrest.

b. **Use an appropriate mode to communicate.** There are various ways to put across a message. A great leader will understand which one is appropriate to address a given situation or audience.

- Song. Africa is a continent rich in *expression,* where repetitive songs are a critical part of communication. At birth, we do songs for a naming ceremony, at initiation we do songs to call for bravery, at marriage we do songs to teach matters of sex, handling of a man; at political rallies we do political songs, at funerals we do dirges, and at worship we do songs in praise of the Almighty. A great leader will, thus, know the song to invoke at a given event so that what he or she intends to communicate is magnified by the song.

- A story. Stories were common in old Africa and were used to *communicate* great lessons of life to the young, but they remain just as potent today. A wise head of state with an unpalatable message to pass to the nation may invoke the use of a relevant story to say what needs to be said without coming out in black and white.

- A proverb. This is a wise saying that drives a point home based on experience. One of the greatest ones is this: *One who eats alone cannot discuss the taste of food with others.* The Swahili people, of East Africa, have this one: *Asiye sikia la mku, huvunjika guu* – He who does not obey elders will break a leg. Proverbs remain a very powerful tool of communication, but they require handling by an experienced, credible voice. The head of state, the leader of a church and the CEO are all welcome to use proverbs to communicate if by so doing, a message will be passed that needs to be handled with a lot of care.

- Hyperbole. Hyperboles are exaggerations *designed* to pass a message by *blowing* a matter out of proportion. A cooperate head would be forgiven for blowing *projections* by saying his company's revenue will jump by fifty to sixty percent when in reality the firm only anticipates revenue increase of a modest fifteen to twenty percent. This is meant to rally the troops. A head of state may call citizens to action by promising an economic growth-rate of ten percent where only three percent is feasible. A church leader may fire up his troops by pointing at a village and warning that all its inhabitants will be won to Christ and baptized in just one year of evangelism – a feat unachievable by anyone but one meant to call people to action. A great leader will communicate through this tricky medium without coming out as oddly unrealistic or even a liar.

c. **Understand the nature of a situation.** A leader is greatly undermined by appearing irrelevant as he or she communicates. Relevance is evidenced by:

- Tone used. In a visit to Africa, Pope Francis made friends among the continent's poor by the tone he used as he addressed their plight. Through a *soft smile*, genuine laughter and right words, he rebuked in love when he had to; uplifted the *spirits* of the suffering masses when he had to; and condemned evils like corruption, murder and civil wars when he had to. His tone spoke of love and the warmest care. Great leadership is about adopting the right tone as one speaks with those he or she leads.

- Facial *expressions* used. In the United States, one of the fixtures that has always drawn my attention is the presidential debate for those seeking nomination of either the Republican or the Democratic ticket. As the debate rages, the facial expression of those under attack speaks volumes about the way they regard the attack and the attacker. When a leader speaks, those he or she leads will always study the face that goes with the words – because expressions never lie. They say what the words have failed to convey.

- Body language. The other word for this is deportment. Along with facial expressions, it says what words have forgotten to say. Fidgeting, folded hands, looking down and drawing with the toe say much more about what's going on in the mind than what one actually says. In leadership, it is crucial to ensure that what the face, the body and the actual words says are in *coordinated* harmony so that the message intended to be passed is conveyed by *synchrony* of *the person*. When a leader speaks, the totality of his or her being must be deployed in the act of *communicating* so that ONE message is heard – not many.

d. **Know the facts.** Imagine that you were the chief executive officer of a top corporation. Imagine that a report was dropped on your desk about a serious matter, but you failed to read it. Imagine that when the time came to make a decision you called all workers together and started to address the matter at hand only for employees to realize you were not on the same page with them – the matter you were now addressing was resolved two weeks earlier and those who needed to be reprimanded had been reprimanded. The *cluelessness* is not only *embarrassing*, but it demonstrates a troubling sense of being out of touch. This undermines credibility because it creates the sense that the leader is asleep on the job and the company can do without him or her. A great leader is one who is keyed in on each aspect of a company's operations and knows the facts before he or she gets up to address employees.

Communicating Hope

On the Friday morning I sat down to think deeply about communication, ahead of writing this book, I *prayed* about the subject matter because I realized the weight of it. I knew that communication was the *medium* through which souls were won or lost; the *bridge* that great leaders crossed in order to convey a message of hope to the people they led. I sensed that after the fall, the only role of leadership is to restore man to a loving and saving relationship with God and that the only way that can be done is through communication. It makes or breaks!

In the years I have served as a pastor and a Bishop of Redeemed Gospel Church, I have counseled with leaders in all segments of society. The urgent cry of the corporate, church and government leader is the same – how do I get people to believe in my vision? What these leaders are actually asking is: how do I get the people I lead to believe in restoration? How do I inspire hope in them?

Anointed leadership comes equipped with the power to read the world well and to instinctively know what, how and when to communicate a message that brings hope by its promise to restore order and calmness. Whether it is a strike at school, an epidemic in a vast region, a coup in a nation or a precipitous decline in profits, what people want to know is not how educated a leader is, how well-connected a leader has managed to become, but how he or she intends to restore order and calmness. The leader is supposed to promise hope and spell out measures to be taken to achieve that feat.

The message of hope the world needs to hear – after man has endured years of tragedy in the world – was given when Christ was perched on a cloud, bound for heaven. The disciples stood there distraught, stunned that the Lord was leaving for real. As Christ watched them, He sensed they needed a word of encouragement. In that moment of great significance for Christendom, the Son of

God reached deep in His heart and pulled out words that came to be called the Great Commission:

> Go therefore and make disciples of all the nations, baptizing them in the name of the Father and of the Son and of the Holy Spirit, [20] teaching them to observe all things that I have commanded you; and lo, I am with you always, *even* to the end of the age." Amen (Matthew 20:19-20, KJV).

Similar sentiments were expressed by the Prophet Isaiah when it appeared the Israelites needed a word of hope. In words reminiscent of God's rhetorical questions to Job, the hurting people of Israel were drawn back to the path of faith by questions – which culminate in the Lord's *promise* to be with them. Listen to this:

> Fear thou not; for I am with thee: be not dismayed; for I am thy God: I will strengthen thee; yea, I will help thee; yea, I will uphold thee with the right hand of my righteousness (Isaiah 40:10, KJV).

This is the amazing message of hope Africa and the world needs to hear today. In a continent beset by wars, hunger, diseases and hopelessness, the President, the Pastor, the CEO and the Chancellor need to tell the people they lead to *fear not* – because the Lord is in control.

That Friday morning, as I reflected on this chapter, I felt a chill when it occurred to me that for all of us who God has called to leadership, the ultimate test of our loyalty and success will be how well we communicated the coming restoration when Christ returns. We will be judged by the hope we spread to those we were called to lead by *pointing* them to the great Messiah who heals all wounds. On that sunny morning, I came to understand communication as the only mechanism God has given leaders to help His suffering children look past the desolation around them to the coming day of wiped tears and restored glory.

The Power of Silence

Christ's studious silence as He stood before Pontius Pilate made those who were around feel haunted and humiliated. The Roman leader felt compelled to ask a few questions to acquaint himself with the *background* of the accusations leveled with hate and anger against Christ, but rather than answer, Christ kept quiet (Matthew 27:11-13, NKJV).

The world has been treated to the specter of leaders who have a loose tongue and will speak many words that cause neither comfort nor enrich hope. Great leaders have learnt the art of silence and know how to use it to achieve great results in their leadership. Most leaders in Africa – in all spheres of life – would do well to learn this art.

There are critical situations, however, when silence could be perceived as arrogance, haughtiness or even being out of touch, but for the most part it is seen as a matter of principle when used by a credible, trusted leader.

The Lord has anointed and wired leaders for His children. They are the men and women who will know when to talk and when not to. They follow in the footsteps of Christ by listening to the voice of the Holy Spirit, which tells them when it is time to speak and when it is time to remain silent. And as we have already noted, *silence only means silence* when body language, facial expression and words all come together to communicate by saying nothing.

Earth's Final Communication

It will be a loud trumpet sound, followed by the voice of the archangel. As recorded in 1st Thessalonians 4:16, in the New King James Version, the dead in Christ shall rise to meet Him in the air.

> For the Lord himself will come down from heaven, with a loud **command**, with the **voice** of the archangel and with the **trumpet** call of God, and the dead in Christ will rise first (bold emphasis mine).

This will mark the end of all communication on earth. The world will plunge into darkness as all systems will shut down to give way to final restoration – that glorious event that will signify the culmination of years of seeking to bring back the *redemptive rule of God* on earth.

The greatest day in the life of a leader is the day he or she discovers that communication is the only tool given to those anointed, designed to help them point each person on earth to that coming day of full *restoration*. The saddest day in the life of a leader is the day he or she forgets this.

TEN

PRAYER

Most leadership books I have read appear to attach little or no significance at all to prayer. They treat prayer as a suspect activity and find no place for it in the leadership of today's complex companies, churches or nations. I find it curious that the more man appears to need the wisdom of the Creator – the one who knows everything – the more leaders despise and walk away from God. In an effort to preserve *accolades* to themselves for successes, such leaders position themselves to absorb all the glory and never to mention the Creator who provided the wisdom, health and strength for successes achieved.

In Hollywood, one of the most anticipated nights of all is the night of the Oscar awards. Directors and actors look forward to it because it affirms one's successes and makes him or her earn the deep respect and admiration of peers. On that night, though, the world has been treated to the bizarre specter of actors and directors who get to the podium and praise everyone – from my mama to my friends and cast of the winning movie – but never God. In their thanksgiving, God does not feature. If He does at all, He is a footnote – either mentioned first to get Him out of the way or last to remain politically correct. The most important player in success is the one least appreciated.

In this book, we have endeavored to remain politically incorrect and have discussed the bold issues in leadership from the *point of view* of the only LEADER there has ever been – the one from whom His servants on earth derive power to preside over the affairs of nations, churches and companies. We have retrieved the subject matter from the firm grip of actors in the demonic world who seized it and redefined it to suit their whims.

These are the conniving *forces of darkness* that have baptized leadership in worldly philosophy and taken away God from its center. They have carefully and steadily made us comfortable with godlessness in leadership and caused professors to point fingers at anyone who seems inclined to put God at the center of it all. It would indeed appear that in the United States and other Western nations, the effort has *succeeded*. Progressives and Liberals have made it a big issue to worship at school or call upon the name of the Lord in public. They appear uncomfortable with God and make it seem cool to be anti-God.

I am not competent to discuss, at length, the motivations that goad a nation founded on liberty and the desire to worship to forget its foundation of prayer, but I know that Africa cannot afford the games the West is playing. I know that great leadership in Africa is achieved on bended knees rather than in an upright posture. Prayer is the most urgent and most powerful tool in the hands of a leader because it is the language God understands.

Prayer Defined

Within the context of this book, prayer has to be defined as the channel through which an earthly servant-leader is connected to the source of power in heaven. It is the *toolkit* a leader needs to access the grace and favor required to lead God's children to safety in an unsafe world; to prosperity in a poverty-stricken world; to wholesome greatness in a world that defines greatness by raunchiness and the loudest abuse of the Creator.

While on earth, Christ gave His disciples a model prayer because He knew they would need it. His desire was to unveil a form of prayer that touched on all aspects of life *at once*. In what became known as the Lord's Prayer, He told them that when you pray, say these words:

> Our Father which art in heaven, Hallowed be thy
> name. Thy kingdom come. Thy will be done, as in
> heaven, so in earth. ³ Give us day by day our daily
> bread. ⁴ And forgive us our sins; for we also forgive
> every one that is indebted to us. And lead us not into
> temptation; but deliver us from evil (Luke 11:2-4, KJV).

Other versions add the words: *For thine is the kingdom, the power, the glory, forever and ever.* In an earlier chapter, we discussed the importance of this prayer in the life of a leader. When a leader of a nation asks the Lord to bring upon his or her nation the exact circumstances prevailing in heaven at any given moment, the leader is seeking blessings upon the people by asking that diseases, poverty and wars be eliminated … in Jesus name. When the leader of a corporation asks that what's in heaven be brought into his company, the leader is pleading with the owner of all resources to look upon the company with favor. When a church leader says thy will be done on earth as in heaven, the leader is asking God to usher the glory of worship into the hearts of those he or she leads.

Each morning, as leaders wake up in Africa – and around the world – they have no excuse to get to the gym, to the kitchen, to the next meeting or fly out of the nation for talks in a foreign nation without seeking God's guidance through prayer. The burden Africans have carried through the years is lack of prayer in the State House. Leaders have turned those sanctified places into chambers for plots and fun rather than places of worship. They have schemed evil rather than sought the Lord as a partner in watching over His own people.

I come from the school of thought that believes each one of us has been given the ability to pray, to seek the Lord on a personal level. There is nothing I have, for example, that the Lord has not given you when it comes to prayer. The only difference is in our understanding of God and the reason He has placed us here. A deep understanding of that mission will expose us to prayer's core principles.

a. **Knowledge of God.** There is *intellectual* knowledge and *experiential* knowledge. Intellectual knowledge is the shallow form that makes philosophers and scholars of times past and present talk about God in abstract terms, caging Him in the prison of past deities that have ceased to have relevance in the world today. Experiential knowledge is the form that abides in deep faith in God because the one who has it has walked closely with God and can attest to His unfailing faithfulness. Knowing God goes beyond knowing His names:

- Yahweh
- Jehovah
- Allah
- Almighty
- Omnipotent
- The Ancient of Days

To know God is to *wake up* with Him, *to go through the day* with Him, to *go back to bed* with Him. It is the act of staying connected, through prayer, with Him in all our endeavors and watch as He pulls us through storms unscathed. Great leaders are those who have discovered this secret. They have come to realize that the winds and the waves obey His will and peace prevails when He is in the boat.

b. **Understanding the dangers.** The reason we have to remain connected – at all times, through prayer, to God – is because we are up against an adversary who seeks, at each turn, to destroy us, steal from us or kill us. As leaders, we have to understand the grave dangers God's children face in epidemics, in civil wars, in collapsing companies, in doctrinal isms and even in confusing philosophies. In his letter to the Ephesians, the Apostle Paul warned that: *For we wrestle not against flesh and blood, but against* *principalities, against powers, against the rulers of the darkness of this world, against spiritual wickedness in high places* (Ephesians 6:12, KJV). With the care of a shepherd, the Lord calls upon leaders to steer His sheep away from danger and the paths of unrighteousness. The newest dangers in Africa include:

- Syncretism. This is the amalgamation or the *attempted amalgamation* or fusion of different religions, cultures, or schools of thought. It mixes God's eternal values with the shifting values inspired by demonic agents. In that mix, the values of eternity are lost as God's pure ways lose their power to save.

- Civilian coups. At one time, the greatest danger in Africa was the cold war, which was fought on this land as the United States and the USSR sought supremacy in ideology and expansion of global allies. Today danger has morphed into the grim prospect of civilian coups, where the military top brass pick a favored civilian and installs him or her as the leader regardless of the outcome of an election. If election results play to the script of the military, well and good; if they do not, the military will manipulate those results to achieve its desired effect – a cold prospect that always leads to war.

- Greater wealth. In Africa, *real wealth* started to show up in the last half of the twentieth century and is ongoing. As the continent continues to experience wealth-creation, the lifestyle in Africa is rapidly changing as rich people emulate the West in dressing, eating, worship and entertainment. Immorality and other *abominable* forms of evil have become commonplace as money is deployed in the pursuit of personal aggrandizement. There is no greater danger to the soul than that of seeking pleasure in the world.

c. **Understanding the times.** We live in the very last days of the earth's history. In these last days, the forces of good and those of evil have upped their game, realizing that time won't last long. We have entered the days of the final stretch in a campaign that started soon after the fall. The candidates in this captivating drama of the ages have deployed all resources in a bid to win as many souls as possible. In Christ's case, the great effort is to draw as many people into the fold of safety as possible. In Satan's case, the effort is to lure as many people to the snare of death so that when the time comes, he will face hellfire with millions of those he led astray. In leadership, prayer is about understanding that the times are perilous and can only be navigated safely on the knees. Prayer must be the final answer!

The greatest prayer of Africa should be that the Lord will usher in a new generation of leaders who know Him and understand the nature of the times we live in. Whether in the church, state or business, the continent cries out for the hand of men and women who will lead with their knees on the ground and their heart in the heavens. From Cairo to Johannesburg, Djibouti to Sierra Leone, Africa must lift her voice in fervent prayer for leaders who will transform this into a land of worship.

Persistence in Prayer

Whenever I travel in Africa, I sometimes get this feeling that people have given up on God. The civil wars witnessed in Rwanda, in Burundi, in Angola and Uganda; the famines witnessed in Ethiopia, in northern Kenya and in Uganda; the epidemics witnessed in Ebola-ravaged Liberia, HIV-AIDS and other devastating ailments have made Africans wonder about the power of prayer – about its ability to save lives. Many people have asked why they should pray when God appears to have forgotten Africa a long time ago.

Christ foresaw this despair and answered it.

> You don't know what you are asking," Jesus said. "Can you drink the cup I drink or be baptized with the baptism I am baptized with? (10:38).

Not knowing what we are asking has been Africa's greatest drawback in prayer. We are in the habit of asking all the wrong things. Like these disciples, selfishness is at the center of the petitions we bring before God. We seek glory, pleasure and wealth – not to worship God – but to show ourselves worthy before men. Our *empty* prayers are a disgrace and do not rise to the throne of grace, where they could be answered with urgency.

The Lord's desire is that we should examine ourselves before we pray. The Head of State needs to look deep in his or her heart to determine whether there is a lingering sin of hate, corruption, embezzlement of state resources or nepotism that may stand in the way of answered prayer. It is only after these distracting matters are dealt with that one is finally able to offer meaningful prayer. Prayer, thus, becomes the conduit through which we endeavor to show ourselves blameless before the Creator. It is the medium that goads us to *partner* with God to experience *righteousness* by remaining attached to Him. But it is not a quick fix. In an age of instant coffee, instant banking and instant sex, many of us are tempted to seek instant answers to prayer. Not so, the Lord warns. Be like the widow when you pray, He says. And what did the widow do?

> Then Jesus told his disciples a parable to show them that they should always pray and not give up. [2] He said: "In a certain town there was a judge who neither feared God nor cared what people thought. [3] And there was a widow in that town who kept coming to him with the plea, 'Grant me justice against my adversary.'
>
> [4] "For some time he refused. But finally he said to himself, 'Even though I don't fear God or care what people think, [5] yet because this widow keeps bothering me, I will see that she gets justice, so that she won't eventually come and attack me!'"
>
> [6] And the Lord said, "Listen to what the unjust judge says. [7] And will not God bring about justice for his chosen ones, who cry out to him day and night? Will he keep putting them off? [8] I tell you, he will see that they get justice, and quickly. However, when the Son of

Man comes, will he find faith on the earth? (Luke 18:1-8, NIV)

African leaders have to come to the place where they seek the Lord in persistence to shower grace upon the people. Like the widow, the Head of State has to pray for national security, stability and prosperity; the church leader has to pray for unity in the body of Christ and doctrinal purity; the corporate leader has to pray for *greater* wealth-creation and the use of that wealth to draw people to Christ. All prayer must be done within the context of persistence and faith – so that it is the Lord's prerogative to decide what He grants and what He denies for our sake.

Prayer as a Language of Heaven

Here in my native Kenya, the United States Embassy is located in Nairobi. That embassy is a sovereign territory, where all matters discussed pertain to the United States and the language *spoken* is one understood only within the context and corridors of that nation's operations. Indeed, the scrambled words spoken are designed to be codes that shield *sensitive information* from falling into the hands of the enemies of the United States.

In other words, as the State Department communicates its interests in Nairobi and issues relevant directives on how its *diplomatic* officials in Nairobi should handle the Kenyan government, care has to be taken to use only an approved coded language accessible to these privileged officials. It is a language that serves the exclusive interests of the United States and that nation alone.

Prayer acts in much the same way. As Christians, we are ambassadors of heaven here on earth. We have to be in the habit of speaking in the language of heaven so that our words will not be available for *enemy forces* to decode and harm us. Intercepted communication between us and God is a possibility when we *speak* rather than *pray*. The words off our lips may be used – when they are intercepted by enemies – to curse the favor we are seeking so that the favor never comes, but if it does, it comes as a curse.

This is the reason the only one we must speak with in our hours of joy and peril is God – and only through prayer, the language of heaven – rather than a brother, a sister or a parent. Prayer keeps the deep secrets we share with God secret, making it possible to have a confidant in the most powerful being in the universe. It makes each of us have the ability to share our fears and joys with the *only* father we all share as members of a human race – God. I can't imagine anything greater.

African leadership – in the twenty first century – has to be about having a deep relationship with God, characterized by a palpable sense that prayer is the secret weapon of leadership in the days we live in. It is the cable that must keep heads of state, leaders of churches and heads of corporations plugged to the source of power that will also act as the channel through which the blessings of favor and grace are showered upon the people of God.

Purpose of Prayer

One cool afternoon in Machakos, after we had attended the morning service and people had lunch, we assembled in the sanctuary to discuss prayer. In the spirit of respect for matters divine, most people "strayed" safely within the established boundaries of correct teachings on prayer. Nobody wanted to be *perceived* as a heretic or an unbeliever in such a forum.

As we were about to wind up the session, however, one elderly man, apparently unwilling to keep carrying the heavy burden of self-deceit, put up his hand and said he had to talk. Something had been bothering him a lot, he warned. "Being that people continue to die, diseases are everywhere and corruption is no longer even a matter to be frowned upon … why do we have to pray? Is there a reason to bother with prayer?"

I was glad when he was done asking and he sat down, not because I didn't like the question, but because I felt the Lord had used him to bring up a matter that troubled many folks but they were afraid to ask. His real question was: what is the purpose of prayer? What good does it serve in a wounded, broken world?

Several hands shot up, the enthusiasm of which I judged to mean they wanted to shut him down, give rehearsed answers about *faith* and *faithfulness*. I let a few of the more energized ones talk first. The last of them said, "If we did not pray at all, it would be the equivalent of surrender; of telling Satan he had won and God had lost." As I finally took the question on, I realized that nothing short of a broad explanation would save the day. The people in that sanctuary needed to know why we prayed. The reasons stunned everyone, including myself:

    a. Thanksgiving. King David was an avid psalmist, a leading poet who excelled in weaving poetic lines to praise the Lord. In Psalms 136, he amplified the very essence of thanksgiving by pointing out the confounding reasons God deserves praise. Here are a few of his memorable lines: *O give thanks unto the* LORD; *for he is good: for his mercy endureth for ever.* *2 O give thanks unto the God of gods: for his mercy endureth* *for ever. ³O give thanks to the Lord of lords: for his mercy endureth for ever. ⁴To him who alone doeth great wonders: for his mercy endureth for ever. ⁵To him that by wisdom made the heavens: for his mercy endureth for ever. ⁶To him that stretched out the earth above the waters: for his mercy endureth for ever. ⁷To him that made great lights: for his mercy endureth for ever: ⁸The sun to rule by day: for his mercy endureth for ever: ⁹The moon and stars to rule by night: for his mercy endureth for ever* (KJV). The Lord is to be praised because He is God. He is to be worshiped.

b. Burdens. We have discussed burdens in Africa at length in this narrative. The truth is – burdens are a global phenomenon and no one is spared. As we pray, we are to bring our burdens to the foot of the cross and leave them there. Whether they are lack of school fees, illness in the family, death of a loved one or lack of food to eat. Nothing is too small that it can't be brought to the Lord in prayer; and nothing is too big that He cannot handle it. The Head of State, by virtue of his or her office, has bigger burdens to bring to the foot of the cross – like economic growth, ethnic harmony, political stability, end of corruption, and even spiritual revival in the nation. The church leader has the great burden of keeping God's people on the path of faithfulness. If one sheep should be lost, he or she is to leave the rest in safety and go out to seek the one. The corporate leader has the burden of praying for continued growth of the company so that through its profits, workers and the nation may be beneficiaries of products assembled at the company's assembly plants.

c. **Connection to source of power.** The source of power is the Lord, the Creator of the universe. He is the socket all cables have to be plugged to so that power flows in and through us. Wisdom in leadership is to know this deep secret about the role of prayer as connection to the power source. Africa is in the hunt for leaders who *understand* the role of contemplative prayer in decision-making. We crave leadership that moves only after seeking power and wisdom from God on how to go forward – especially when a matter is as grave as war.

Prayer unleashes upon leaders the wisdom of heaven, causing even the weakest among us to become great. It constantly reminds leaders that there is a Higher Power on whose behalf we are leading. I'm aware that there has never been a study on the relationship between prayerful leadership and performance, but if this were to be conducted, I have no doubt the world would realize that prayer provides balance on a scale nothing else can. It makes leaders come to terms with their place in the great battle to save souls – a battle that will rage till Christ will decisively put an end to it on that glorious day of vindication.

In an increasingly democratizing Africa, the Lord is opening space for Africans to elect only leaders who know Him and understand the incredible power of prayer. We may not go the way of theocratic rule, but we certainly have to up the game in the quality of men and women we allow anywhere near the levers of state power. The cheap gimmicks of voting along tribal lines, religious lines or social class lines have to give way to voting patterns that reflect maturity founded in prayer. The Lord is faithful and willing to partner with Africans in the great search for men and women who will lead not just for today, but for eternity. These are the vessels He will use to close the history of painful existence on earth. He will use these prayerful leaders to prepare His people for transition from this realm below to a higher realm – to full restoration of glory. As a leader prays, so will a nation prosper!

ELEVEN
LEGACY

Mother Teresa, 26 August 1910 to 5th September 1997, also known as Blessed Teresa of Calcutta, MC, was a Catholic religious figure and a missionary. She was born in Skopje, in the Republic of Macedonia, then part of the Kosovo Vilayet, in the Ottoman, into a humble Kosovar Albanian family. After having lived in Macedonia for some eighteen years, she moved to Ireland and then to India, where she lived for most of her life.

Mother Teresa founded Missionaries of Charity, a Roman Catholic religious congregation, which in 2012 consisted of over 4,500 sisters and was active in 133 countries. Today Missionaries of Charity runs *hospices* and homes for people with HIV-AIDS, leprosy and tuberculosis. It also runs soup kitchens; dispensaries and clinics. Members adhere to the vows of chastity, poverty, and obedience, as well as a fourth vow – to give "wholehearted free service to the poorest of the poor."

A controversial figure both during her life and after her death, Mother Teresa was widely admired by many for her charitable works, but was also criticized, particularly for opposing contraception and for substandard conditions in the hospices for which she was responsible. Before she died, the diminutive Calcutta nun received numerous awards, including the Nobel Peace Prize, honorary citizen of the United States and had a university in Tamil Nadu named in her honor.

The world responded to her inspiring love for the poor.

In her simplicity she has been made great.

The subject matter of *legacy* may be discussed without ever mentioning Mother Teresa, but it is made much richer – and even more authentic – by presenting her life as the quintessential life of one who has left a strong legacy. Legacy has been dismissed by certain leaders around the world as a burden relevant only for historians to carry, but it is at the heart of factors that should cause each one of us sleepless nights – when we are in leadership.

Today, when one looks at me, it is easy to tell that the best days of my life on earth now lie behind. Whatever the Lord called me to do on earth is done. I have won many souls to Christ, helped found a body of Christ known as Redeemed Gospel Church and led our *church* in Machakos to build sanctuaries and Maturity Center.

I started the fellowship center because it occurred to me that the original vision of a united body of Christ, which we had when we started the Evangelical movement, had slowly died out, replaced by *denominational separatism*. The center was thus designed to foster that spirit of Christian togetherness and whoever walked away from its spirit of unity or attempted to change the nature of its mission was cursed. Our church in Machakos has started hospitals, schools and other social facilities, but Maturity Center is the greatest vision of my ministry.

May it live on!

Indeed, in the years to come, way after I will have bowed out of the scene, church historians will take a measure of what was done when I was on earth and will establish the scale of my legacy based on evidence of my work. I will be judged on the quality of souls I touched and interacted with: Bishop Lai, Bishop Muyu, Bishop Tuimising, Bishop Masika, Reverend Ibrahim Omondi,; Bishop Matheka – and the redeeming ideas I originated and have impacted those I left behind. While this goes on, I will have left the scene and will lack any ability to change thought on my image. My legacy will have been cast in stone by my death.

Legacy Defined

This is one of the richest words in *English*, with the ability to analyze the life of a human being and pack it into the core image the person has lived – for good or for bad. To illustrate this, we have to work with *examples*. What comes to mind when you think of:

a. **Margaret H. Thatcher.** Margaret Hilda Thatcher, Baroness Thatcher, LG, OM, PC, FRS (née Roberts, 13 October 1925 – 8 April 2013) was a British politician, and was Prime Minister of the United Kingdom from 1979 to 1990, and the Leader of the Conservative Party from 1975 to 1990. She was the longest-serving British Prime Minister of the 20th century and is currently the only woman to have held that high office. A Soviet journalist dubbed her **the Iron Lady,** a fitting nickname that at once became associated with her **uncompromising** politics and leadership style. As Prime Minister, she implemented policies that have come to be known as Thatcherism *(Wikipedia,* bold emphasis mine). Uncompromising toughness!

b. **Mahatma Gandhi.** Mohandas Karamchand Gandhi, 2 October 1869 – 30 January 1948, was the preeminent leader of the freedom movement in his native India. Employing **nonviolent civil disobedience,** Gandhi led India to independence and inspired movements for civil rights and freedom across the world. The honorific Mahatma – or high-souled or venerable – applied to him first in 1914 in South Africa, is now used worldwide. He is also called Bapu, a Gujarati term for endearment as father. In common parlance, in Bharat (India), he is called Gandhiji since reference as Gandhi can be considered lacking in good form and respect (*Wikipedia*, bold emphasis mine).

c. **Nelson Mandela.** Nelson Rolihlahla Mandela, 18 July 1918 – 5 December 2013, was a South African anti-apartheid revolutionary, politician, and philanthropist who served as President of South Africa from 1994 to 1999. He was the country's first black chief executive, and the first elected in a fully representative democratic election. His government focused on dismantling the legacy of apartheid through tackling institutionalized racism and **fostering racial reconciliation**. Politically an African nationalist and democratic socialist, Mandela served as President of the ANC party from 1991 to 1997. He was also the Secretary General of the Non-Aligned Movement from 1998 to 1999 (*Wikipedia*, bold emphasis mine).

Those three are great legacies indeed. They are a positive way to remember the three great leaders of the twentieth century. But just as there are positive legacies, there are negative ones as well. The world has witnessed ruthlessness, betrayal and other forms of evil that have defined perpetrators as such. Their legacies have been tainted and nobody wants to speak of them as heroes – they have been treated as villains.

d. **Pol Pot.** Pol Pot (Khmer), 19 May 1925 – 15 April 1998, born Saloth Sar, was a Cambodian revolutionary who led the Khmer Rouge from 1963 until 1997. From 1963 to 1981, he served as the General Secretary of the Communist Party of Kampuchea. As such, he became the leader of Cambodia on 17 April 1975, when his forces captured Phnom Penh. From 1976 to 1979, he also served as the prime minister of Democratic Kampuchea. The **deeply ruthless man** presided over a totalitarian dictatorship, in which his government made urban dwellers move to the countryside to work in collective and on forced labor projects. The combined effects of summary **executions, strenuous working conditions, malnutrition and poor medical care caused the deaths of approximately 25 percent of the Cambodian population.** In all, an estimated 1 to 3 million people, out of a population of slightly over 8 million, died due to the policies of his four-year premiership (*Wikipedia*, bold emphasis mine).

e. **Hissène Habré** (Arabic), born 13 September 1942, is a former Chadian dictator who was the leader of Chad from 1982 until he was deposed in 1990. Human rights groups hold Habré responsible for the **killing of thousands of people**, but the exact number is unknown. Killings included **massacres** against ethnic groups in the south (1984), against the Hadjerai (1987), and against the Zaghawa (1989). Human Rights Watch charged him with having authorized tens of thousands of political murders and physical torture (*Wikipedia*, bold emphasis mine).

Legacy, as we have demonstrated, can go either way. It is defined by those who have been left behind – after one is no longer alive – to objectively assess his or her impact in the world. Though it takes into account the entire life of a person, it zeroes in on the area in which the person has left an indelible mark on the lives of those left behind. It defines one, in death, as having been a positive influence or a negative influence, thus shaping people's view of the parted for as long as life shall be – and could be even into eternity. Perhaps it was in realization of this scary prospect that many of us cringed when asked how history would one day judge our actions.

Shaping Legacy in Childhood

There is a view gaining currency that legacy is not defined by how one has lived his or her life, but by how the end has impacted earlier life and altered perception of it. At the heart of this argument is that people should not be held accountable for actions taken when they were young or not directly in control of circumstances around them. A child, an adolescent or even young adult, according to proponents of this view, should not be judged on the basis of actions taken while executing the plans of other people in their life. At a certain level, this appears to make sense, but it also has the ability to make people act in silly ways, aware they will be judged only on what transpires once they are older or in a responsible position in society.

I sympathize with those who have not had a chance to meaningfully shape a legacy while young. These are people who, because of circumstances that hindered positive growth, stumbled along till they came to the point where more direct control of life opened a channel for their real character and intentions in life to emerge. Once they could help it, they lived highly productive and responsible lives, impacting others in ways they never could have when they didn't have an avenue to do so.

Legacy, however, is shaped *early* and *maintained* – nurtured through the years like a sore back. Removal of stains from it demands that each stumble is met with determination to take appropriate corrective measures; and that a strong desire to maintain a clean image remains active in one's life. Inevitably, this has to begin as soon as a child is able to make judgment as to what is right and what is wrong. Aware of the need for children to shape their reputation at an early age, Christ urged parents to:

> But Jesus said, Suffer little children, and forbid them not, to come unto me: for of such is the kingdom of heaven (Matthew 19:14, KJV).

The point Christ is making – even to us today – is that legacy is shaped early. Whereas it is called reputation when one is young, or when we are still alive, death releases each of us to the realm where reputation becomes a legacy. When a child dies, his or her reputation quickly turns into a legacy as mourners reflect of a life well lived or wasted in cruelty, carelessness or drunkenness. By saying *let the little children come unto me*, Christ is pleading with parents to guide the children to Him at an early age so that their impressionistic minds can be shaped by Him.

There are those who believe anointed leaders were chosen young and were wired to understand the concept of legacy in childhood. They believe that such anointed leaders lived their life in school, in church, in the playground and at home aware of the need to maintain a good reputation. Where there were conflicts, such leaders restored peace; where there was hunger, they brought relief; and where there were tears, they wiped them away.

They lived the spirit of anointment!

The other point Christ made, by saying *let the children come,* was this: parents are *directly* responsible for their children's behavior and outcome in life. Responsible parenting is to know how many children one may have in relation to the resources available to give them the best in life.

In Africa, we have witnessed the sad situation where the rural poor bring into the world more children than they can take care of. These children end up recycling poverty as they are unable to make anything meaningful of their life. *Let them come unto me,* Christ says.

I wonder what they tell Him about us once patched safely on his lap.

Shaping Legacy as a Young Adult

The story of Joseph is recorded in the book of Genesis 37. The young Jewish boy had a dream about a coat of many colors – and later about his brothers' wheat bowing to his. The dream so displeased his brothers that they sold him to merchants on their way to Egypt. Out there, the Lord filled him with *favor* and he grew up into a handsome man. When Potiphar, the wife of Pharaoh, saw how good-looking he was, she made advances. Joseph declined her wickedness, which made the king's wife tear off his tunic and accuse him of attempted rape.

The matter was investigated and the lies of the evil woman uncovered. Later, because of Joseph's *faithfulness*, the Lord lifted him up and he became a leader in Egypt. One day, his exhausted brothers showed up in Egypt to look for grains because the times were hard back home. There, in fulfillment of his earlier dream, the brothers bowed to Joseph as they asked for help. It was Joseph's moment to avenge their betrayal, once he realized who they were, but rather than do so, he gave them grains and asked them to come back with their father and brother Benjamin. It was on that second trip that when Joseph saw his father and brother, he broke down and revealed who he was.

The brothers were filled with fear.

"I won't harm you," he said.

He embraced them … tears flowing.

Tears of joy!

The rest of the gripping story is in Genesis 37, as I have already pointed out. It is a story that was told to *successive generations* of Jewish adolescents and continues to be told to the youth worldwide in an effort to instill *moral discipline* in them. Joseph's reputation as a moral young man grew in the kingdom and made him be viewed as a reliable man who could be trusted with power. This was a case of an anointed leader being shielded through the snares erected by Satan and his agents to corrupt his soul.

In adolescence, we have all developed into beings capable of making right decisions. Our faculties have reached the point where they work in coordinated harmony to shape our worldview and cause us to live within the safe limits of what society accepts as *right* – not what it rejects as *wrong*. Anointed leaders will go through the *tricky* moments of life much like Joseph did in the palace, when Potiphar came calling – for the rest of God's children, He has given the Holy Spirit as a shield to fend off the arrows of illicit sex, devil worship, drunkenness, substance abuse and even disrespect of parents. The Lord is in the *business* of making us pure in heart so that such purity shapes our legacy.

The point is – should one die in adolescence, the sum of his or her reputation in childhood and adolescence will be tied together to make legacy. In a world reeling under the weight of influences from Hollywood, adolescence has become the most perilous developmental stage for young people. *Impressionistic* and undergoing *physiological* changes that cause the body to react in strange ways, they easily fall prey to tendencies that can be ruinous and defining. Two of the wisest men that ever lived realized the danger of youth and talked to the youth of all ages.

    a. **David.** A man the Lord said was so close to His own heart assessed the world around him and said: *The law of the LORD is perfect, converting the soul: the testimony of the LORD is sure, making wise the simple. [8]The statutes of the LORD are right, rejoicing the heart: the commandment of the LORD is pure, enlightening the eyes. [9]The fear of the LORD is clean, enduring for ever: the judgments of the LORD are true and righteous altogether. [10]More to be desired are they* *than gold, yea, than much fine gold: sweeter also than honey and the honeycomb* (Psalms 19:7-10, KJV).

b. Solomon. He is regarded as the wisest man that has ever lived. Some decisions made in the world today, if they are clothed in wisdom, are regarded as *solomonic*. Writing to the youth in the book of Ecclesiastes 12:1, (NIV), he issued what amounted to a warning: *Remember your Creator in the days of your youth, before the days of trouble come and the years approach when you will say, "I find no pleasure in them."*

The manner in which a young adult carries him or herself in college will play a critical role in shaping legacy. This is the place in life where the nature of interaction one has with members of the opposite sex, books, worship and sports separates those who will go on to be leaders from those who will become followers. At this level, leadership has begun to reveal itself in people and it isn't uncommon to hear professors and other concerned authorities make the judgment that a certain student will go on to become great. The wiring for greatness has come to be seen.

Indeed, from this point on, society holds the view that *each* person is old and knows enough to be held accountable for his or her actions. As one later evolves into an adult and engages society as its employed member – or as an entrepreneur – reputation becomes a key player in how people judge the person. At work, as in other key places, people seek reference to help them determine the kind of person they are dealing with – a good or a bad guy?

It is also credible to imagine that by this stage, leadership qualities have strongly emerged and society is beginning to take note. In politics, one may begin to hear people calling on him or her to run for office. In the corporate world, one may begin to hear employees asking him or her to consider becoming the new CEO upon retirement of the outgoing one. In church circles, one may begin to hear parishioners asking that he adds his name to the list of those seeking election as the new bishop.

As the young people of Africa go forward, aware many of us have been called to leadership, we must find solace in the timely advice of David in Psalm 46:1-3 (NIV).

God is our refuge and strength,
an ever-present help in trouble.
[2] Therefore we will not fear, though the earth give way
and the mountains fall into the heart of the sea,
[3] though its waters roar and foam
and the mountains quake with their surging.

In adolescence and young adulthood, Joseph's life is our guide. By being faithful in the little things God gives us, He pours His favor upon us so that we become the vessels He will use when the time comes. Africa is in dire need of Josephs as the Lord prepares us for greatness. The continent needs men and women whose moral uprightness is not the subject of debate, but the subject of awe. This is the way great nations are birthed.

Legacy in Leadership

This is the place we have been coming to in this chapter. The leaders we opened this chapter with – the three great ones and the two evil ones – shaped their legacy once in office by the actions they took to affect the lives of the people they led. The key elements we are to consider in determining the scope of a legacy are:

   a. **Vision.** Visionary leadership is true leadership. It is made of a strong idea that guides the evolvement of policy so that the direction a movement, firm, nation or church takes leads to greatness. Nelson Mandela's vision of a united, prosperous South Africa continues to shape the destiny of the nation and will one day become a key plank of his legacy should South Africa become a cohesive society along the lines of his vision. Thatcherism has gone on to define conservative politics in the United Kingdom years after the departure of Baroness Thatcher from the scene. And in India, Gandhi's vision of a prosperous, peaceful nation shapes the manner the economic giant is engaging in foreign policy and is digging a deep foundation for market economics. These are powerful visions whose positive impact on people continues to define their legacies as leaders who were called.

b. **Impact on people.** The horrible impact of Pol Pot's murderous reign is still felt in Cambodia. Idi Amin Dada's misadventures in Uganda remain a sore part of the nation's history. In Chad, the ruthlessness of deposed dictator Hissène Habré continues to be felt as the central African nation goes from one ruinous civil war to another. Great leaders leave behind a legacy of strong nations that prosper after they have left the scene.

c. **New nurtured leadership.** A great leader is aware of the need to mentor new leadership. He or she is aware that for policies and vision to remain on course, they have to be left in the hands of men and women who:

- Share the vision. Those who share the core tenets of the vision will ensure that policies are enacted that steer a movement in the direction of harmony with the vision. The goals and culture established will be left in place as long as they serve the greater good of moving the entity toward its vision.

- Have energy. Energy may also be viewed as passion. In a world where leading people has become so challenging, it takes passion to keep going – even in the face of strong opposition. A leader who leaves his legacy in the hands of weaklings has set in place a system that will *undo* that legacy. The leader will have unwittingly shot self in the foot.

- Understand the stakes. In African political leadership, the stakes are *driven much higher* than in other world regions because of the volatility of ethnic mix on the continent. A great African leader – in politics, church or the corporate world – will understand the grim danger of civil war and act to keep passions low for the sake of peace.

Across Africa, it is difficult to point at credible examples of great legacies – in church, state or the corporate world. Of course there are many unsung heroes and heroines, but as one scans the landscape for public greatness, there are but a few personalities to credibly work with: Nelson Mandela, Desmond Tutu, Julius Nyerere, Aliko Dangote, James Mwangi, Ellen Sirleaf Johnson, and Joyce Banda. These are some of the handful of men and women who have impacted people's lives positively and have acted as role models for the young.

It would appear, based on the list, that Africa has given the world fewer heroes than other regions have. In a new brave world that showcases leaders with *inspiring legacies* in academia, in corporate management, in military prowess, in church shepherding and in medicine, our motherland showcases mediocre legacies and curves its tail under the belly with shame where greatness is celebrated.

The trail of assassination, ineptness, nepotism, bloodshed and corruption that has dogged the continent has to cease as we march deeper into the twenty first century. This land is ripe for the leadership of men and women who will leave behind legacies worthy of the land that sheltered Christ as a toddler when a king wanted to kill Him. We have to become the home of peace and prosperity as the Lord raises anointed servants with clean hands and even cleaner hearts. That is the legacy promised to the people of Africa if we shall – in one accord – go on our knees to seek the Lord's help in ridding Africa of despots and replacing them with those anointed to follow in the safe footsteps of the Creator, the only LEADER the universe can trust to do *only* what is good for us.

EPILOGUE
UBUNTU

As I look deep into the future of Africa, what I see is a land that will be led by men and women who embrace the philosophy of *Ubuntu*. This is a philosophy fashioned out of the biblical concept of love thy neighbor as you love thyself. It presupposes that the king can only be a king because there are subjects; and the subjects can only be subjects because there is a king. The interdependence we experience because of caring for one another is what makes us human and is what the Lord wants to *characterize* our relationships here on earth – especially at a time we are under the attack of the powers of darkness. We are called to be our brother's keeper until Christ returns.

Given the state of affairs in Africa, where systems are weak and the world remains disinterested in black issues, leadership has to be of a different nature compared to other parts of the world. African leadership has to work toward restoration of hope, uplifting of human dignity and pointing people to the worship of God. It has to return the people of Africa to the plan God had for them when He placed this continent in the heart of the world.

The divine plan was to set up a land of worship, a glorious realm from where attacks would be launched on territories conquered by Satan and his demonic agents. Leaders on the continent were to act in accordance with the Laws of God as they led the world in restoring the glory of the Eden down here. Our leaders were to enjoy the blessings of the land Christ chose to hide in by creating many more sanctuaries where the broken, hurting children of God would hide from despots and evil rulers out there.

Satan knew of this plan.

And went on the attack.

He destroyed it.

Instead of Africa being that glorious land, it has become the land of pain and tears. It has become a desperate continent ravaged by civil wars, epidemics, assassinations, famine and inept leadership. State Houses and palaces that were supposed to become staging grounds for sending missionaries to lands beyond the seas have instead become bastions of *ungodly* worship, where strange rituals are entertained and our heritage subverted on a daily basis. They have become shrines used by the enemy to spread the diabolical gospel of a covenant sealed through the blood of hate and competition with God.

In men like Idi Amin Dada, Mobutu, Kony and deposed Chadian strongman Hissène Habré, Satan has advanced his cause in Africa on a scale that has left the continent in a state of weakness. The African nation is wounded – *but I dare say not mortally*. The time has come for the last crop of leaders to take their place in Africa. These are they who have been raised to restore Africa's lost glory as the home of the Lord's people fleeing persecutions around the world. The continent is about to regain her place as the land of freedom in worship and thought.

With this new designation, the Lord has poured His spirit in the land to awaken our conscience. We are to be led to the new realm, where the sanctity of time and life are of the greatest concern to anointed leaders in the church, in the state and in our corporations. The veil of darkness that has hovered over Africa is about to be lifted and replaced by the white robe of purity as leaders fix their gaze on the shepherd of the flock, the mighty Jehovah who has been, is now, and will always be.

As Africa prepares to meet Her bride, we are called upon to prepare for the feast that has been prepared since the days of the fall. The past has been painful, but the future will be glorious. May the African State House, the African Church and the African Corporate Headquarters bow to the LEADER of the ages, Him who set leadership to last *from the Eden to Eternity.*

> Now unto him that is able to do exceeding abundantly above all that we ask or think, according to the power that worketh in us, 21Unto him be glory in the church by Christ Jesus throughout all ages, world without end. Amen (Ephesians 3:20-21, KJV).

TESTIMONIALS

In the late 70s, I relocated to Machakos to work at the Standard Bank. I needed someone at that time in my spiritual life to father me. Having been saved in high school, I didn't have a spiritual father. I had been praying for God to give me one.

One day I went to a small hall behind the Machakos Hospital, where I had been told there was a Bible Study slated for the day. I went after work and there was nobody. I found a man praying on his belly, with his head on a dusty floor. As I sat on a bench, the Lord whispered to me that *he is your father, serve him.* I went home and began to pray for him every evening.

I later started a prayer meeting in my house, which became very popular. Some leaders in the church fueled a rumor that I was starting a church. One evening, Bishop Mutua came to see what was going on. He waited to see the nature of our interaction, but we only prayed and people left. We never gathered to say anything. It was just prayer. After everyone left, I came out of my bedroom to lock up.

I found Bishop Mutua all alone in the living room. He greeted me and asked if I was the one who worked at the bank. I told him I was and he told me about the rumor he had heard that I was starting a church. "If what I have seen here is what you are starting, I will also be a member," he said. It was the first time we met. For the next five years, as I worked in Machakos, I became a member of Redeemed Gospel Church Eastleigh.

It was from there that God called me to full-time ministry.

The bishop has since been a father to me and I have never shied away from calling him Dad. He has been a great encouragement in tough times. I have known him as a man of integrity. I come to him for his words of wisdom.

You will know a father cares for you when he calls you aside to warn that you were getting late in finding a lady to marry. I had just ended a great sermon in Machakos when the Bishop came to me and asked for a moment. As we huddled at a corner to speak, he didn't beat about the bush. He asked why I had allowed myself to get as old as I was without a wife.

Bishop Dr. Lai, Jesus Celebration Center, Mombasa

———

In the years I have been lucky to know and interact with Bishop Mutua, I have admired him as a humble servant of the Lord. He has led by example – reaching out to younger ministers and Christians whenever we needed him. He kept himself accessible and showed us what it meant to balance family life and leadership.

In our family, Reverend Agnes Masika and I have looked up to him and his dear wife, Gertrude, for inspiration. From them we have learnt how to offer Christ-centered leadership in an age of moral relativism, spiritual decline and strange philosophies founded on suspect theologies of the modern age.

The Evangelical Movement in Kenya remains strong because of his role in establishing a strong foundation upon which its Scripture-based theology is built. In spite of challenges the church faces today – and may face in the future – we are not to be shaken because we have a guiding light in the path trodden by this patriarch.

Bishop Titus Masika, Founder and Director Christian Impact Mission

———

It was a privilege to meet Bishop Paul Mutua in 1973 at Machakos High School. He had escaped from Uganda at the time of the great persecution of the church by Idi Amin. He was living with Rev. Johnstone Kiseve, who worked and was housed at the school.

During those days, when he did not know what to do or where to begin, he spent many hours lying in the grass and praying. Those were difficult days for him because not many people knew him or his ministry in this country. The interesting thing was that he did not appear like a man in trouble.

It was during those difficult days that we got to know what kind of a man he was. As young high school boys on fire, we decided to organise a Christian camp in the school. The principal of the school allowed us to hold a Christian camp meeting in our school. The Lord provided all that we needed. The only challenge we had was that we did not have preachers for the seven-day camp There were not many preachers in those days. We requested Bishop Mutua to be one of our speakers even though we did not know him.

He graciously accepted.

So we had two mature speakers – Bishop Mutua and Rev. Kiseve.

We started holding special intercession meetings for the first soul-winning camp. Seeing the way this man of God prayed provoked us to seek the Lord more urgently. We had a very powerful move of the spirit during that first camp meeting. That is when we saw Bishop Mutua deliver the gospel with power and great dedication.

We had a father figure with us.

The presence of Bishop Mutua brought the necessary balance to that camp and even future meeting and ministries. As young people in ministry, he became a reference point to us. He warned us when carried away by youthful excesses after being used by God. He rebuked us in love. I owe much of what I am to this man of God. We took him in as a father in the soul-winning ministry and also in our lives as individuals.

I worked closely with him in the formative years of the Redeemed Gospel Church, where he was the Deputy Chairman and I was the Executive Secretary. During those years, I saw a man who hated controversy and sought peace with all people.

This is a man that trusts the Lord to meet his needs and has never used tricks to get money from people. He has kept the faith, enduring great hardships with a lot of patience. He provoked those of us who were close to him to a life of passion for God, devotion to the cause of the cross, endurance in tribulations and most importantly, to a life of integrity.

His life is a book that should be read by all!

Bishop Mutua's life cuts across denominational barriers. He is a father and a mentor to many. The anointing upon his life has touched many lives in the country and other nations of the world.

Join me in celebrating this great hero of faith!

Bishop Peter Sila, The Living Word Church

ACKNOWLEDGEMENTS

I thank God for the powerful partnership of my wife Gertrude and our children, which has enabled me to be a humbled shepherd for more than five decades. May the Lord reward you!

I'm indebted to Pastor Peter Kyengo and Professor Philip Kitui, they who sat with me for many hours to interrogate my thoughts on leadership and capture my life history for posterity.

I'm grateful to the Church faithful in the Pentecostal movement in Kenya for keeping the faith through the years. The remaining journey is long, but we are already conquerors.

I praise God for Sam and Hellen Okello of Sahel Publishing Association for guiding me through the publishing process and producing a world class book. May the Lord reward you and grow your ministry for His glory.

ATTRIBUTION

The author of *Leadership From Eden to Eternity*, Bishop Paul Mutua, is indebted to *Wikipedia*, whose content he has used to form portions of the narrative in this book.

All Bible texts are from the KJV unless otherwise mentioned.

**Editor, Sahel Publishing Association,
Nairobi, Kenya**

www.ingramcontent.com/pod-product-compliance
Lightning Source LLC
Chambersburg PA
CBHW030923090426
42737CB00007B/305